Jailhouse Glock

A Garcia Girls Mystery

LIZBETH LIPPERMAN

This is a work of fiction. Names, characters, places, brands, media, and incidents are either the product of the author's imagination or are used fictitiously, and any resemblance to actual persons, living or dead, business establishments, events, or locales is entirely coincidental.

For more information, please direct your correspondence to:
The Story Vault
c/o Marketing Department
364 Patteson Drive, #228
Morgantown, WV 26505-3202

JAILHOUSE GLOCK
A Garcia Girls Mystery

http://www.lizlipperman.com

ISBN-13: 978-1533018205
ISBN-10: 1533018200

Second Edition

Cover Design by Kelly Crimi
Interior Book Design by Bob Houston eBook Formatting

Published by The Story Vault
Website: www.thestoryvault.com

Dedication

To my sisters, Lill, Mary Ann, Dorothy, and Theresa, who died way too young. Without you, I couldn't have written this book around the loving relationships between the Garcia Sisters.

Acknowledgements

To Dan and my children and grandchildren who never cease to brighten every day for me.

To my amazing agent, Christine Witthohn, who is my biggest cheerleader and task master. I couldn't do this without her.

To my critique partner, Joni Sauer-Folger, and to my beta readers, Sylvia Rochester and Chris Keniston, all talented authors themselves, for making me a better writer.

Chapter One

"**G**ive me ten minutes with that sweet body of yours, and I promise you'll be begging for mercy."

Madelyn Castillo shoved the graham crackers and milk through the opening, never bothering to glance up at Gino Bernardi. Since she'd come on duty three hours ago, the man had been running at the mouth about how he could improve her sex life.

What sex life? She'd officially turned into an old maid, preferring that over dating any day. At least considering the dates she'd had in the last few years. This loser was definitely not a step up.

"How about tomorrow night I buy you the biggest steak in Dallas?" Bernardi's grin widened as he picked up the snack and sat down on the edge of the cot in the corner of his cell. "And then show you that orgasm," he added with a leering glance at her chest.

"I'd rather eat rattlesnake," Maddy fired back, eyeing him suspiciously. "What makes you think you'll be out of here by tomorrow night, anyway?"

Bernardi smiled. "Let's be real. We both know I'd already be eating leftover turkey if my freakin' lawyer hadn't picked this weekend to fly to the Bahamas."

"Don't be so sure. Your luck may have run out this time." She glanced up. "You roughed up that guy in the bar pretty good. Lucky for you, he's okay."

"He started it," Bernardi said, sounding much like a little kid caught fighting with a younger brother. "I was minding my own damn business until that mother grabbed my girlfriend's ass. He's lucky I didn't kill him." He stood and approached the bars. "How come you didn't haul his ugly mug down here?"

"We did." Maddy pointed to the adjoining cell where Alan Foxworthy was lying on the cot facing the wall, his snores loud enough to penetrate the wall between the prisoners. "He's here sleeping it off. Like you should be doing."

"Yeah, right. Why would I want to do that when I can have you in here with me? You'd have to work hard to make me forget my Chrissy, though. That bitch is a freaking contortionist." He flashed his pearly whites. "Are you up for the challenge?" he asked before taking a huge bite of the cracker. "All those beers have my diabetes acting up. I always get a humongous boner when my sugar's up."

Maddy ignored him and walked to the next cell to check on Foxworthy. Curled in a ball on his cot, his soft snore was loud and rhythmic. Fortunately, the guy had only suffered a swollen right eye and a small cut on his upper lip along with some bruised ribs when he'd tangled with Bernardi.

"Come on, pretty thing, 'Save A Horse, (Ride A Cowboy') like the song says."

Give me a break.

Number one, Gino Bernardi would never be mistaken for a cowboy in his designer jeans and silk shirt, and number two, she hadn't ridden a horse in years, around about the same time she'd actually ridden a cowboy.

She was beginning to regret coming to work tonight. Her measly salary was so not worth having to babysit an obnoxious perv like Gino Bernardi. Most days she didn't have to deal with his kind. Still trying to wrap up her last few college credits at night school, she normally worked the morning shift. Tonight she'd offered to switch with Jeff Flanagan so he could enjoy his kids over the Thanksgiving holidays. Something had come up unexpectedly, and his ex had asked him to keep them overnight.

She had a soft spot for kids and their daddies, especially since her own ten-year old had never seen hers. With Jessie at her grandmother's for the weekend, Maddy had volunteered to take Flanagan's shift.

She jumped when Bernardi slid the empty tray through the opening. "Sugar, I swear I've never seen a police woman who looks like you, and trust me, I've seen plenty of them. You could be the cover on one of them naked cop calendars." He lowered his voice. "And just between you and me, I'm about to become a rich man. If you treat me right, I might be tempted to spend a little of it on you."

Maddy frowned as she pulled the tray through. "Try to get some sleep, Bernardi. I'll be out front if you need anything."

He smirked. "Oh, I need something, all right. And you do, too, if you'd ever admit it. Come on. Ten minutes. That's all I need." When she started toward the door, he called after her. "Okay, five minutes."

Just shoot the sonofabitch and put him out of his misery.

Maddy screamed, jumping back as the tray clattered to the concrete floor. "Tessa! What are you doing here?"

"Who's Tessa?" Bernardi asked, leaning as far as he could to see through the bars. "Maybe we can do a three-way."

Sounds good, big boy. Why don't you go ahead and get started? Slip into something more comfortable—like a coma!

Maddy blinked twice, then ran from the cell area. She lowered her body into her chair, letting out the breath she'd held while she ran. She had to quit burning the candle at both ends. Even her mind was starting to go just like the rest of her stressed-out body.

Surprised to see me, sis?

Maddy shot straight up when her younger sister plopped down on the edge of the desk. Her *dead* younger sister! "It's really you?"

In the flesh, Tessa said, her eyes scanning the empty police station, before settling back on Maddy. *Okay, maybe not in the flesh, but here, nonetheless.*

Maddy tried to calm down enough to think rationally. "Why are you still here? I thought you were finally at rest after we found your killer."

Yeah, you may have found him, but he got off too easy when Colt put a bullet in his back. The SOB didn't suffer nearly enough.

Maddy sighed. "Would you have preferred that he kill our sister instead? Colt did what he had to do to save Lainey." She poked her finger toward her sister but felt only air.

Give it up, Maddy. You can't feel me.

"Thought you'd gone off to wherever dead people go for eternal peace, or whatever."

Yeah, that eternal peace thing is overrated, if you ask me. Tessa sniffed. *I was sent back to help you.*

"Help me with what?"

Beats the heck out of me. I just go where they send me. Tessa giggled. *St. Peter's old lady wanted me out of there in a hurry.*

Despite herself, Maddy laughed. Her younger sister had always had a penchant for pissing off other women, usually over a man. But St. Peter? She didn't even want to know what Tessa had done. "So, really, why are you back? You told Lainey your work here was finished."

I know. I know. Like I said, I have no idea why I'm here. Tessa scooted off the desk and walked around to face Maddy. *What'd you go and do?*

"Nothing," Maddy said, indignantly. "My life's fine. My daughter's fine."

How is that sweet niece of mine?

"Jessie's good," Maddy answered, finally allowing her shoulders to relax.

Seeing her dead sister had been quite a shock but not totally a surprise. When Tessa was poisoned the year before, she'd come back to help find her killer. At first, Maddy and her three sisters had freaked out, but they'd finally accepted it to be true when Tessa began spouting off secrets only she could have known. Back then, Lainey was the only one who could see or hear the ghost, and they'd all assumed Tessa had gone off to the big condo in the sky when her murder was solved.

"You look good," Maddy finally managed to say.

I do, don't I? No wonder that old bag didn't want me around Pete. Tessa's grin faded, and she eyed Maddy curiously. *Are you sure you're not in trouble?*

"Positive." That's if you overlooked the fact that she had gone through all the money from Robbie's life insurance. Or if you didn't know that she was already two weeks late on her house payment.

A year ago when Colt asked if she had any aspirations of being a police officer, she hadn't thought twice about it. But giving up the better-paying job as station office manager for a rookie cop's pay had taken its toll. She and Jess had just moved from their tiny apartment into the old Krieger house right down the street. She'd sunk a ton of money into renovations before her paychecks took a dive, but the remodeling had turned out better than she'd hoped.

Then the air conditioner went out about the same time the waterline under the house sprang a leak. She'd had to dig deep to meet the expenses, and it was a no-brainer that they'd have to sacrifice eating out to build that emergency fund back up. Given her culinary skills, she and her daughter would be microwaving a lot of frozen dinners for the foreseeable future.

"Really, Tessa, I'm fine. I love it that you've come back to check on me, though." Maddy tried to sound flippant, but she couldn't stop the bad feeling from welling up inside her.

Like I had anything to do with it! Tessa shook her head. *How are the new vines doing?*

"They're growing. After your killer burned down the vineyard, Lainey sent off to Palermo for cuttings identical to the ones that were there. She replanted the entire vineyard and is just waiting for the grapes to grow."

That's good. And how are my sisters?

"Lainey and Colt are trying to get pregnant, and Kate is doing some young stud neurosurgeon who just moved to Vineyard from Canada."

A neurosurgeon, huh? My baby sister makes me proud. Tessa's smile spread across the width of her face before it faded. *Colt deserves a child of his own. I'll always regret letting him believe Gracie was his.*

"Yeah, that was really low, even for you, but it all worked out in the end. Colt's the only father Gracie has ever known, and now that..." Maddy's eyes swiftly made contact with her sister's.

Now that I'm dead and out of the way?

Maddy sighed. "I didn't mean it to sound that way, Tessa, but you gotta admit, you weren't the nicest person walking the planet before you died. You threatened to take Gracie away from him, for God's sake."

Yeah, I was a shit, but I only wanted more time with my daughter. Tessa crossed her legs, exposing gams that were just as shapely as the day she'd died. *Enough about what a low life I was. You never mentioned Deena. How's my other big sister?"*

"You just missed her deadbeat husband. Deena sent him over with enough leftover Thanksgiving food to feed an army. Too bad you can't eat." As if on cue, her stomach growled. She got up and walked to the small refrigerator in the break room before returning to her desk with the glittery insulated lunch carrier Mike had dropped off.

Pretty fancy lunchbox, I have to say. Deena always had an eye for design and was the best cook of all of us.

"Don't you mean the only cook?" Maddy shook her head. "Out of five girls, you'd think Mom would've taught a few more of us how to whip up those great Mexican enchiladas she used to make."

You were always too busy trying to get Robbie Castillo to notice you, I was chasing every rich guy in Vineyard, and Lainey and Kate had their noses in books all the time. Deena was the only one who showed any interest, which by the way, might not have been such a good thing. Last time I saw her I thought for sure one of her seams was gonna pop. What's up with that?

Maddy shrugged. "I don't know. Between living with that loser of a husband and working with the witch who runs the nursing home, I think she turns to food for comfort."

Lainey warned her not to marry that jerk almost up to the day she said, 'I do.' But she wouldn't listen, even after Lainey told her about seeing Mike with another woman in Ruby's Café. She clucked her tongue. *What kind of idiot flaunts a girlfriend in his fiancé's favorite restaurant?*

"Deena only saw the good in him. Said he was just having pre-marital jitters. Even now she still looks the other way."

That boy would be kissing his joystick goodbye if he was married to me.

Just then, a loud rendition of *Girls Just Wanna Have Fun* pierced the quiet of the room. Maddy's eyes shifted toward Tessa, unable to squelch the apprehension that suddenly washed over her. She glanced down to the source of the music and slowly opened the desk drawer. A cell phone skittered across the bottom as it vibrated.

Taking a deep breath, she scolded herself for being so paranoid. She picked up the phone and flipped it open, ready to razz one of the guys for leaving it at the office. She'd bet money it belonged to Landers. The kid would forget his head if it wasn't screwed on.

"Looking for your phone?" Maddy asked with a laugh.

"Madelyn Castillo?" the voice on the other end asked.

"Yes," she stammered, not recognizing the weird voice as any of her co-workers. Silently, she prayed her sister's sudden appearance was only a mistake.

"Checked on your daughter lately?" the computer-enhanced voice continued.

Panic set in the minute Jessie was mentioned. "Who is this?"

"You might want to take a look at the text messages."

Maddy jerked the phone from her ear and held it out in front of her as she pounded the menu button. Her fingers were shaking so badly she hit the wrong one twice before finally getting to the right page. The minute she clicked on the massage, a photo popped up. "Oh my God!" she said, almost inaudibly as she dropped the phone on the desk.

Tessa leaned over and stared at the picture, her facial expression turning serious as she viewed the image of a hooded man standing over Jessie's bed, a gun pointed directly at her head.

Find out what they want.

Chapter Two

"**I**'ll kill you if you touch her," Maddy screamed into the phone instead. She envisioned what they might do to her daughter and giant tears streamed down her cheeks. "I don't have much money, but whatever I have, it's yours," she pleaded.

"We don't want your money."

"Then what? I don't have anything of value."

"First of all, let me make myself perfectly clear. If you tell anyone about this or call in your cop friends, your daughter will never see the light—"

"I won't," Maddy interrupted. "Just don't hurt her." Her voice cracked.

"Her chances of seeing the sun rise tomorrow depend entirely on how you cooperate with us. All you have to do is put this cell phone along with your own phone, your gun, and the keys to the cells in the back room on the desk, then go into the lady's bathroom. Lock the door and wait fifteen minutes. If you do that, your daughter will never know we were here. If not..."

Maddy's mind raced. Were these Bernardi's friends coming to get him out? The last few times the man had been arrested for drunk and disorderly, his lawyer had posted bail before the ink had a chance to dry on the sign-in sheet. Or maybe it wasn't Bernardi they wanted to spring. Maybe it was the other guy. He wasn't a local. Was it possible they were looking for something in the police station? If so, what? And how did they know Jessie was at her grandmother's?

"What's it gonna be, Madelyn?"

The distorted voice jarred her back to the critical decision she had to make. She was way out of her league here. *Good Lord!* She'd only been an actual cop for three months.

In a flash, Maddy made the decision. She opened the bottom drawer and pulled out her purse. She had to call her brother-in-law. Colt had been the head of Vineyard's police department for many years and would know what to do. "How can I be sure you won't hurt her?" she asked, hoping to stall while she frantically searched for her cell phone.

"You don't," the voice replied. "It's a gamble you have to take, but if I were you, I wouldn't be stupid enough to call anyone on that cell phone you're digging for."

Maddy dropped the purse with a thud, her eyes scanning the room, coming to rest on the security camera in the corner. Flanagan said it had gone on the fritz earlier that day, and the company was sending someone up from Dallas in the morning to fix it. The red light was off. So how did he know what she was doing?

"That's right, Madelyn. I can see everything, so it wouldn't be real smart to jack with me." He paused before adding, "Unless, of course you prefer living alone."

She covered her mouth to stifle the sob welling up in her throat. This was not a spur-of-the-moment breakout. This guy had planned every detail. Gino must have friends in high places.

"Tessa?" Maddy did a three sixty, but her sister was gone. She was all alone and talking to a potential kidnapper. Or worse.

"I'm waiting, Madelyn."

Maddy blew out a breath. This was a no-brainer. Her daughter was a helluva lot more important than making sure some slick gangster wannabe stayed locked up for the weekend. When his lawyer returned on Monday, he'd be sprung faster than an over wound clock anyway.

"When do you want me to do this?"

"Now would be good. My guy at Gramma's house is just about due for a fix, and he always gets major jitters when that happens. Wouldn't want his trigger finger shaking. Know what I mean?"

She pulled the cell phone out of her purse and slammed it on the desk along with the other one she'd been using. Reaching across her body, she unholstered her Glock and placed it next to the phones. After a final glance around the room failed to turn up the location of another camera anywhere, she unlocked the main door and sprinted to the bathroom.

Once the door closed, she searched for something she could use as a weapon just in case the caller had more on his mind than freeing Bernardi. She spotted a mop in the corner, cursing under her breath at her vulnerability without a gun. But she'd had no choice.

She grabbed the mop and crouched in the corner behind the door. If someone did come in, at least she would have the element of surprise.

Unless there's a camera in here, too.

She did a quick scan but saw nothing out of the ordinary. The smell of Clorox mixed with mildew caused her nose to crinkle, and she pushed the mop away from her body.

Good heavens! Don't they ever clean these things?

Minutes passed with no sound, and Maddy was beginning to believe one of the guys would pop in, laughing his butt off. Rookie cops always got harassed, and she was due. She wondered who it would be? Flanagan? Rogers? Most likely candidate was Danny Landers. He was the practical jokester of the station. Probably called the minute he finished the sweet potato pie at his folk's house.

Let's just see who surprises who, Danny boy, she thought. It wouldn't be so funny when the mop connected with his crotch, and she sure as hell was going to make sure it did. It would serve him right.

She stiffened her back against the cold tiled wall when she heard a faint sound on the other side of the door. Leaning closer, she listened to the muffled voices.

Probably Danny and the other guys getting ready to march in and scare the crap out of me. She tightened her grip on the mop.

Please God, let it be Landers. A twisting in her gut told her it wasn't.

Then a loud shot rang out, followed quickly by two more. Maddy jumped up from her corner, nearly tripping over the mop. She pushed at the door, giving no thought to what danger lurked on the other side.

It didn't budge.

She lowered her shoulder and jammed it into the door again.

This time she was able to open it enough to squeeze through past her desk that had been shoved against the door.

Raising the mop in an offensive position, she made her way to where the desk had been, aware her every move was probably being watched. She spied the keys to the cells lying in the middle of the floor next to her cell phone, but there was no sign of the other phone or her gun.

An icy chill sliced through her body. She needed a weapon, and she needed it now. She raced to Colt's office where she knew he kept a forty-five locked in the bottom drawer. Trembling, she felt under the desk for the key taped behind the leg, and when her fingers touched it, she ripped it from its hiding place and quickly opened the drawer.

With the gun finally in her hand, she made her way to the back room, taking a deep breath and slowly exhaling. A quick glance at the camera into the cell area revealed nothing unusual, yet, a sudden sense of overwhelming doom washed over her.

The minute she opened the door, she tried to convince herself the shots were only fired to scare her. Halfway to Bernardi's cell, she knew they weren't.

Charging through the already opened steel door, she felt the nausea bubbling in her throat when she saw a man's body sprawled on the concrete floor, a crimson river flowing beside him. She bent down and rolled him over, unable to stop her scream as she stared into the eyes of a very dead Gino Bernardi. She felt for his carotid, hoping to find a pulse, knowing she wouldn't.

Jumping up, she moved to the next cell only to see the other prisoner in a sitting position against the wall, his county-issue orange jumpsuit sporting a growing red ring. Two fingers on his neck revealed a pulse, weak and racing but still there.

Running from the cell, she reached for the phone on Landers's desk. After telling the 911 operator to send an ambulance ASAP, she called her mother-in-law, her fingers now shaking so badly she could barely dial the number.

After several rings, a sleepy voice answered.

"Sandra, where's Jessie?" Somehow she managed to sound semi-calm despite the ball of fear churning in her gut.

"Asleep in her bed," Robbie's mother said after hesitating a few minutes. "Maddy, what's the matter?"

"Go check on her!" Tears fell unchecked down Maddy's cheeks. "Now!" She tried to slow her respirations with deep slow breaths, but the silence on the other end was maddening.

"She's sound asleep. Maddy, what's going on?" Sandra repeated, her voice escalating an octave.

"Wake her up," Maddy commanded. By the time her mother-in-law came back on the phone, she'd already made several bargains with God.

"Hi, Mom." Jessie's sleepy voice was like music to Maddy's ears. "Nana said you wanted to talk to me."

"Oh, God, Jess. Are you alright?" Maddy heard the child's sharp intake of breath as she yawned.

"Why wouldn't I be?"

Maddy stifled the cry that threatened to escape her lips. No use terrifying her child. "Tell your grandmother to take you to her bedroom and lock the door. I'm calling Tom Rogers now and having him swing by the house to take a look. Don't come out of the bedroom until he says it's okay."

"Maddy?" Sandra apparently grabbed the phone from her granddaughter. "What's going on?"

Maddy repeated the command, adding, "It's probably nothing. I'll tell you about it when I talk to you after Rogers checks out the house. Keep the door locked. Do you still hide a key under the flower pot on the patio?"

"Yes."

"Good. I'll let Rogers know. Stay in the room until you hear from me."

Maddy found Tom Rogers at the diner and related the story. She hung up just as the paramedics charged into the station with a stretcher. Her mind racing, she watched them assess the wounded man in the cell next to Bernardi and start an IV. When he was on his way to County Hospital, she remembered she hadn't called Colt and dialed his number using the phone on Landers's desk.

"Maddy, what's wrong?" The concern in Colt's voice was apparent. A call from the police station in the middle of the night couldn't be good.

"Colt?" She heard her sister's sleepy voice in the background.

"Bernardi's dead."

"I'm on my way."

The phone rang as soon as she'd disconnected from Colt, sending a shiver of fear up her spine that only intensified when Tom Rogers' name popped up on Caller ID.

She took a deep breath and held it for a few seconds before answering. "Please tell me everything's okay," she begged.

"Other than your daughter and your mother-in-law being scared out of their minds, everything's fine. I've checked all the nooks and crannies in this place and found nothing. No trace of anyone ever being here."

"Thank God," she whispered before lifting her eyes upward and promising to go to church more often.

"Do you want me to come back to the station now?"

"No," she shouted into the receiver. "Stay there until you hear from Colt. He's on his way in now."

She hung up and sat down in Danny Lander's chair. Within minutes she heard the siren from Colt's police car and breathed a sigh of relief. Her brother-in-law would know how to make sense of all this.

She walked back to the cell block and took one more look at Bernardi, noticing that the trail of blood had snaked its way to the wall and puddled. The metallic smell reached her nostrils just as a shiny black object on the edge of his bed caught her eye. Slowly, she walked into the cell, being careful not to step in the blood around the dead man's head.

The nausea resurfaced. Jerking her head around, she puked into the stainless steel sink. The shiny object was a gun. Her Glock.

Chapter Three

Maddy was relieved to see Colton Winslow charge through the station door with her sister Lainey close behind. If anyone could make sense of this horrible situation, it was her brother-in-law. She crumbled into Lainey's embrace while Colt stood to the side, patiently waiting to hear what had happened.

As much as she wanted to stay in the warmth of her sister's arms, she knew the faster Colt had the details, the faster they could begin collecting evidence and find Bernardi's killer. Pulling away, she motioned for him to follow her into the back room where the cell block was located.

Lainey fell into step behind Maddy before Colt held up his arm to stop her. "You'd better stay out here, honey." When she shook her head, he added. "We need someone to direct Mark Lowell to the back when he gets here."

The look on Lainey's face said she clearly wasn't fooled by his suggestion that the medical examiner of Vineyard needed help finding his way to the cell block, and for a minute, Maddy thought she would protest. With an exasperated sigh, Lainey nodded.

Her younger sister had never seen a dead body before, and she probably would have nightmares forever if she saw Bernardi. Maddy was a cop, but she'd only seen one other body herself. She shuddered at the memory of old Mrs. Roosevelt who had died in her sleep. Ordinarily, it wouldn't have required police presence before the funeral home arrived for the body, but her son had insisted that his sister had something to do with his mother's death. Since Maddy had been Flanagan's shadow back then, she'd gone out with him to investigate.

Fortunately, she'd been able to get through the initial ordeal without a major GI disaster. It turned out the son had been right about his sister, and the crime had been solved in less than a week. But she'd never forget the way the old woman's eyes had stared up at her—almost as if she were begging for someone to find her killer. Maddy still had an occasional bad dream about those eyes.

"Maddy, you want to start at the beginning and tell me how this prisoner was shot to death on your watch?" Colt asked as he stared down at the body.

She took a deep breath and blew it out slowly. "I was in the bathroom when it happened."

He walked around Bernardi to the other side of the cell. "There's a Glock next to the body."

"Yes." Her voice dropped to a whisper. "It's mine."

He whirled around to face her. "Thought you said you were in the bathroom."

"Someone shot him while I was in there."

"With your gun?"

A wave of nausea pulsed through her again, knowing how this must look to a trained police officer. "It's a long story, Colt, but you have to believe that I didn't kill him." She swiped at the tear threatening to roll down her cheek.

His face softened, and he stepped closer to her. "Of course, I believe you, but I need help making sense of this. How it is that someone could waltz in here and kill this prisoner with your gun while you were in the ladies' room? And where was Rogers?"

She lowered her head, thinking there was no way she would be able to make him believe her. "Out checking a domestic disturbance call that came in around one from that trailer park by the airport. You know, the one that keeps the guys busy nearly every weekend with drunk and disorderly calls."

She waited until he nodded, deciding not to tell him that Rogers had stopped at the all night diner for a cup of coffee afterward. Everyone knew the divorced cop was sweet on the new waitress who worked the graveyard shift there, but it would serve no purpose bringing that up now. "Anyway, he told me to leave my gun and my cell phone on the desk and to lock myself in the ladies' room."

"Why would Rogers tell you to do that?"

"Not Rogers. The guy on the phone."

Colt's forehead wrinkled in question. "Somebody called you on your cell phone and told you to lock yourself in the bathroom?"

This time she couldn't stop the tears from falling, and she shook her head. "There was another phone in my desk drawer, and when it rang I thought one of the guys was calling to say he'd left it. The voice sounded like it was computer enhanced and—" She stopped to reach for the tissue Colt handed her.

"I don't get it, Maddy. You know the protocol when you're here alone at the station. Why didn't you go into lockdown? You're been here long enough to know you should never leave the front door open with no backup."

"I was so scared."

He wrapped his arms around her until the shaking stopped. "Did he hurt you?"

She shook her head and pulled away. She had to tell him the story before the medical examiner and the forensics team showed up. "He texted a picture of a man with a gun standing over Jessie while she was sleeping at Sandra's. Said if I didn't do exactly as he instructed, he'd kill her."

Colts eyes widened, and he headed for the door. "Call Rogers and tell him to meet me at your mother-in-law's. Tell him to sit tight until I get there."

"Colt, wait!"

He stopped abruptly and spun around to face her.

"Jessie's fine. Rogers is over there now, and other than being scared to death because I freaked out, both my daughter and her grandmother are fine. Actually, they slept right through the whole ordeal, and neither had a clue that someone had been in the house."

Colt blew out an audible sigh of relief. "Thank God for that." Maddy knew he loved Jessie almost as much as he loved his own daughter. Switching back into cop mode, he narrowed his eyes. "Show me the picture. Maybe we can get forensics to pick up on something."

"Like what?"

"Like a tattoo on the hand holding the gun or some other distinguishing mark."

She turned and raced back to the front office with Colt close behind her. Ignoring Lainey's questioning look, she sprinted to her desk, which was still partially obstructing the bathroom door. After going through the drawer, she glanced up and shook her head. "It's gone."

Just then Mark Lowell burst through the front door. "Heard someone saved the taxpayers a lot of money tonight," he said, winking at Colt.

"The body's in the back." Colt sent the Vineyard County Medical Examiner a look that instantly wiped the grin from his face before he twisted around to face Maddy again. "Can you sit over there at Landers's desk while I do the preliminary exam with Mark? I'll be back shortly to take your full statement." He motioned to Lainey. "You too. This place is about to become a zoo, and I'll need both of you out of the way."

"Shouldn't I come with you?" Maddy asked.

His eyes told her more than she wanted to know. No matter how much of her story he believed, she was still a potential suspect—actually, the *only* suspect at the present time.

"Hang tight, Maddy. I promise we'll get to the bottom of this." Then he nudged the medical examiner toward the cell block and disappeared behind him.

Maddy flopped down behind Landers's desk, and her sister pulled up a chair beside her.

"You must've been so scared," Lainey said, reaching for Maddy's hand.

Maddy could only nod. She was the oldest of five sisters, and she'd always been the one to comfort the younger ones. It felt strange being the one needing support right now.

"Who's with Gracie?" was all she could think to say without breaking into tears again. She had to get the image of that man in Jessie's bedroom out of her head.

"She's with Colt's mom tonight. They're braving the Black Friday crowd in the morning."

"I didn't kill him, Lainey. I swear."

Lainey patted her hand. "Why would I think that? You couldn't hurt a flea. Everyone knows that."

I knew you were in trouble, Maddy. I just didn't know how much.

Maddy glanced up to see Tessa sitting on the edge of the desk. "Please tell me you know who did it, Tessa," Maddy said, hoping and praying her ghostly sister had seen everything and could identify the man who had killed Bernardi.

"Tessa? Don't tell me you're seeing her now," Lainey said, jumping from her chair.

"You can't see her?"

Of course she can't. You're the one in big trouble. Tell Lainey I said she could have at least combed her hair. She's got that just been...well, you know the look. And personally, to flaunt it in front of me—-and you, for that matter—- seems a tad insensitive, don't ya think?

"Tessa said you can't see her because I'm the one in trouble." Maddy deliberately left out the other part, not wanting to dwell on the lack of romance in her life at the moment.

A slight grin wrinkled the corners of Lainey's lips. "Knowing my dead sister the way I do, my guess is that's not all she said."

Oh, give it a rest, Lainey. You had your fun with me when you were the only one who could see and hear me. Tessa leaned across the desk, almost in Maddy's face now. *Now start talking, sis. The only way we can help you is if you tell us what happened.*

Maddy felt the hope drain from her body. If Tessa was looking for details, that meant she hadn't seen anything and wouldn't be able to help. She lowered her eyes and recited the story to both her sisters.

"Oh my God! Is Jessie all right?" Lainey cried out.

"She's fine. She slept right through it. Rogers is staying with her until I get home."

Thank God for that, Tessa interjected. *What asshole uses a child like that?*

"Apparently, a very clever one," Maddy answered. "There's only one scenario that would have persuaded me to follow his instructions like I did. He knew Jessie was key to getting my full cooperation."

"Why didn't you call Colt?" Lainey asked.

"I tried to, but somehow, the man on the phone saw me and threatened to kill Jessie."

"How did he see you?" Lainey asked. "Was he hiding in one of the back rooms?"

Maddy popped out of the chair, nearly tipping it over. "Crap! I forgot to tell Colt about that. There has to be a hidden camera somewhere in this room." She started toward the door to the cell block just as it flew open and Colt walked through.

"Get the forensics guy to check this room for a hidden camera," she shouted, unable to hide the excitement in her voice. "Maybe we'll find fingerprints on it."

"What makes you think there's a hidden camera, Maddy? It's a little far fetched to think someone could plant one without any of us knowing about it."

She told him how the man on the phone knew she'd been searching in her purse for her cell phone and how he warned that he could see her every move.

"Like I said, it's very improbable that someone could get eyes on us in here." When he saw her look of despair, he added

"I said improbable, not impossible. But it makes more sense that he made a calculated guess, knowing you'd be looking for help."

Damn! The man looks good even with bedhead. Tessa walked around him, spending a few extra seconds giving his derriere the once-over. *I should have jumped his bones when I had the chance.*

"Tessa's back," Maddy said abruptly. When Colt narrowed his eyes, she added, "She appeared before this all began and disappeared right after I got the call."

"So she didn't see or hear the guy?"

Maddy shook her head. "No, but she knew I was in some kind of trouble." She grinned. "Said St. Peter's wife sent her here to get her as far away from her husband as she could."

"Why am I not surprised?" Colt deadpanned, before his expression turned serious again. "Tell her not to even think about getting involved in this investigation. The last time you Garcia girls tried to help out, Lainey almost died."

Remind my ex that I'm the one who led Lainey out of the burning vines to safety. She clucked her tongue. *I have a feeling this isn't going to be nearly as much fun now that Colt knows I'm hanging around. I liked it better when he couldn't figure out how you guys knew everything.*

"What's going to happen now?" Lainey asked, grabbing her sister's hand and squeezing it. "Surely you don't blame Maddy for doing what she did?"

He stared at his wife for a moment before focusing back on her older sister. "I would've done the exact same thing if someone had threatened Gracie. But because it was your gun that killed Bernardi, I have to put you on leave for now." When he noticed the look of dismay that crossed her face, he added "Paid leave, Maddy. Just until we get to the bottom of this."

She nodded, grateful she wouldn't have to dig any deeper into her savings to make it through the next few weeks. She hoped it wouldn't take any longer, but that meant they'd have to find clues quickly before the case went cold.

"There's really nothing more for you to do here. Why don't you go with Lainey back to our house and try to get some sleep. I'll wait here until the CSI guys are through and the body's on the way to the morgue."

"No!" she said a little louder than she meant to. "I need to be with Jessie."

"That's a good idea. I've already instructed Rogers to stay over at your mother-in-law's house until morning just in case whoever did this decides to return."

"This time I'll be ready," Maddy said defiantly before she remembered her gun was now state's evidence.

I'm going with you, Tessa said. *Nobody screws with my family and gets away with it.*

If the situation hadn't been so serious, Maddy would have laughed as her younger sister slammed her hand on the desk and no one else noticed.

Before she could explain why she was grinning, the phone rang, and Colt stretched across Landers's desk to reach for it. "Vineyard Police Department." After a few seconds of listening, he blew out a breath. "We'll be right there."

Both Maddy and Lainey inched closer to him, waiting for him to explain.

Before he did, he glanced down at his watch. "That was the hospital. Alan Foxworthy has regained consciousness. They're getting him ready for surgery, and I have a short window to talk to him before they sedate him. Hopefully, we can get to the bottom of this quickly."

"What about the station? Should I stay until morning?" Maddy asked.

"No, you go and stay close to Jessie. Landers's on his way in." He bent to kiss her forehead. "Try not to worry too much. I'll call you as soon as I know something."

Even as she agreed, she knew there was no way she would stay calm. Her mind raced with the possible scenarios Colt could get from questioning the guy in the other cell. What if he hadn't seen anything and wasn't able to help her? He was snoring loud enough to nearly shake the building the last time she'd checked on him.

Hope that little bastard has a good memory, Tessa said, falling in step with Maddy as she retrieved her purse and walked to the door.

Exiting the station with Tessa on her heels, Maddy felt a ray of hope for the first time since this all began. Unless the killer shot the other guy before Bernardi, there was no way anyone could have slept through the loud gunshots. Colt would take his statement, and Maddy would be back on the job in a few days.

Climbing into her car, she glanced back at the station. She could only hope that would happen and she could resume her life in short order. She'd left college to marry Robbie before he was deployed to Afghanistan, and when he was killed several months later, she'd found herself pregnant with only the small government compensation to support her and her newborn daughter. She'd worked at the station in some capacity or another ever since Colt took over as sheriff of Vineyard.

But her gut screamed back that walking into the station in her uniform wasn't going to happen anytime soon.

Chapter Four

Even as Colt walked through the Emergency Room door at Vineyard Regional Medical Center, the churning in his stomach didn't ease. If everything went well, in the next few minutes he'd get confirmation from Alan Foxworthy that Maddy had not pulled the trigger. With a little luck, the wounded man might even be able to describe the real killer. Then they could concentrate on getting the police artist's sketch out and nail the bastard who'd held the gun to his favorite niece's head.

Without Foxworthy's statement, all they had to go on was Maddy's word that she didn't kill Bernardi. Her version of how it all went down wasn't the easiest to believe, particularly the part about the anonymous cell phone in her desk drawer—the one that had magically appeared and then just as conveniently disappeared.

But knowing his sister-in-law the way he did, he knew there was no way she could actually kill a man, even one as obnoxious and slimy as Gino Bernardi.

At the thought of the dead man, Colt racked his brain for something—anything--that might give him a clue as to who might have had the balls to pull this off. To walk into his police station and commit premeditated murder with his rookie officer's own gun took a serious set, not to mention the right connections.

But no matter how hard he tried, he came up empty.

All he knew about Bernardi was that he'd moved to Vineyard several months before and hadn't gone out of his way to make friends in the community. Personally, he thought the man to be an arrogant SOB, stupid enough to end up on the cell block at least once or twice a month for some brush with the law, usually a bar fight. The last time he'd occupied one of the cells, Gino had gotten all liquored up and ran his car into a brand-new Porsche owned by Vineyard's only celebrity, a Dallas Cowboys' linebacker who'd apparently cut him off in traffic. Lucky for Gino the cops had gotten to him before the three hundred plus athlete had.

Clearly, Gino Bernardi couldn't hold his liquor and had made more than a few enemies since he'd arrived. But did any of those people he'd managed to piss off hold a big enough grudge or have the clout to methodically plan and execute the perfect hit?

Colt would get his deputies to take a long hard look into Gino's life as soon as he got back to the station. In the meantime, he had a potential witness to interrogate, and hopefully, what the man had to say would make this investigation a whole lot less personal.

He walked up to the front desk where a tired looking, middle-aged woman was on the phone and never even bothered to glance up.

When she finally did, she asked, "You looking for the gunshot victim, Sheriff?"

"Yes."

The woman chugged the last of her coffee before pointing down the hall. "Third room on the right, but you'd better hurry. The OR tech is on his way down from the fifth floor to take him to surgery, and the anesthesiologist will want to give him a little something to take the edge off before they transport him upstairs."

Colt nodded before heading down the hall. The fire in his abdomen upped a notch with each step in that direction.

Why am I so apprehensive about talking to this guy?

He made eye contact with Jeff Flanagan who'd been called in to guard the prisoner and now sat outside the room with an opened newspaper on his lap.

"Has he said anything yet?"

Flanagan shook his head. "We were waiting on you, boss. You don't have much time, though. The doctors think a bullet may have nicked his intestines, and they're anxious to get him into surgery."

Colt took a deep breath and pushed through the doorway. The first thing he noticed was how noisy it was with all the monitors. He'd hated that sound long before becoming a cop. He connected it with a time many years before when his dad lay dying from a hit-and-run accident. As much as he despised the constant beeping, he remembered how much worse he'd felt the moment those sounds had stopped.

He forced himself to walk closer to the bed and waited while the nurse piggybacked a smaller IV bag to the bigger one. When she was gone, he got his first look at the man who could possibly identify the gunman and save Maddy a lot of grief.

Alan Foxworthy wasn't a big man, appearing to be about five-ten or eleven with a nose that could only be described as oversized. Why a man who was a good four inches shorter and fifty pounds lighter than Gino would pick a fight with him was beyond good sense. It was a wonder the drunken Bernardi hadn't killed him during their altercation.

Foxworthy's eyes were closed when Colt approached the bed, but they fluttered open just as he touched the side rail where the man's hand was cuffed to the metal.

"Mr. Foxworthy, I'm Sheriff Winslow. Can you tell me anything about the man who shot you?"

Foxworthy, whose face was still swollen and now a deep shade of purple and red from the beating he'd taken at the bar the night before, looked confused. "Man? Who told you it was a man?" He stopped and winced, grabbing his abdomen as if a sudden pain had shot through him.

"Wasn't it?" Colt took a deep breath. This was not going down the way he'd hoped.

"Hell no. It was that lady cop," the injured man said, his voice almost a whisper now.

A cold sweat began to form on the edge of Colt's forehead. He leaned in closer to hear. "You're sure it was a female cop? Could it be that you just remember the cop being the last person you'd seen before shots were fired?"

Foxworthy winced again, wiggling in pain. "I'll never forget the look on her face when she pointed that gun at me."

He closed his eyes and nodded. "It was the lady cop, all right."

Just then two men in scrubs wheeled in a gurney. The older of the two pushed past Colt. "Sorry. We have to get this man into surgery now." He pulled a syringe from the chest pocket of his scrubs and reached for the IV tubing. "Mr. Foxworthy, this is going to make you sleepy. When you wake up, you'll be in the Recovery Room."

A few seconds later Foxworthy closed his eyes, and the two men moved quickly to slide him from the bed to the stretcher. All Colt could do was watch them transport his only witness out of the room toward the elevator.

Foxworthy's last words replayed in his mind. The man had basically sealed the case for the DA against his sister-in-law, and he'd have to be the one to break the news to her.

In his heart he knew it couldn't have been Maddy. Was it possible someone disguised as her had done the deed? Looking down the barrel of a Glock had to have captured all of Foxworthy's attention, and any woman in a police uniform could have impersonated his only female officer. And hadn't Maddy said the voice on the phone was computer enhanced? It wasn't a huge stretch to entertain the possibility that the killer was a woman, especially after Foxworthy's testimony.

"Well, did you get anything from him?" Flanagan asked when Colt walked out of the room.

"He said it was Maddy."

"What? No way. The scumbag's lying."

"But why?" Colt asked, talking more to himself than to Flanagan. He patted his officer's shoulder. "Stay here until he gets out of surgery. I'll have Landers relieve you then so you can get back to your kids."

Turning, he walked down the hall toward the exit, the fire in his gut reaching volcanic levels. The good people of Vineyard had elected him to bring law and order to their small city. At times it was harder than usual to do just that. But it sickened him that right now he had to live up to the responsibility they'd placed on him.

With a heavy heart, he drove his squad car out of the hospital parking lot and down the road, knowing he was about to arrest a good friend—and a member of his own family—for the murder of Gino Bernardi.

* * * * *

Maddy hurried up the steps of her mother-in-law's house, scanning the area at least three times before reaching the porch, just in case whoever had been there earlier was still hanging around. Satisfied the intruder was probably long gone, she used the key Sandra had given her and opened the door. Before she even made it inside, Jessie ran up and wrapped her arms around her mother's neck.

"Mom, what's wrong? Why did you send Officer Rogers here tonight?" Tears rolled down her cheeks. "You sounded so scared on the phone."

"Shh, sweetheart, I'm fine," Maddy whispered, brushing her daughter's hair back soothingly. "I was worried about you and your grandmother, that's all." She made eye contact first with her mother-in-law and then with Mike Rogers whose face showed his utter confusion about why he'd been asked to stand guard over his coworker's family.

She pushed the ten-year old an arm's length away and kissed her forehead. "It's late, and we've got a big day ahead of us tomorrow." When Jessie's eyebrows arched, she added "We're putting up the Christmas tree, remember?"

That brought a smile to her daughter's face. "Oh, yeah. Come on, Gramma." She grabbed Sandra's hand and bounded up the steps to the bedroom.

Maddy moved closer to Rogers. "You're absolutely sure no one's up there, right?"

He shook his head. "I checked every available inch just like you asked me to. If someone is there, he's invisible." He turned and watched while Jessie closed her bedroom door before focusing his attention back on Maddy. "You want to tell me what this is all about?"

Maddy blew out a long breath, half in relief and half in frustration. "You're not going to believe it." She pointed to the kitchen. "Let's go in there and talk. Jessie's not above sneaking out of her room and listening from the top of the stairs. I'll put on a pot of coffee."

He followed her into Sandra's kitchen and sat down on a barstool at the counter. Silently, Maddy got the pot of coffee brewing before she followed suit. Biting her lower lip, something she always did when she was nervous, she let her eyes wander around the brightly colored kitchen with its lemon-yellow walls that she'd helped her mother-in-law paint not that long ago.

She loved this room, had spent many hours in here with Robbie and his parents while they'd prepared dinner or snacks or sometimes just talked over coffee like she was doing now. God, she wished Robbie was here with her. He'd know how to rub her shoulders and make her feel like things would get better.

But he'd been gone over ten years, and she'd had to learn how to fend for herself.

Robbie Castillo had been an only child, and Sandra and Big Rob, as they'd called Robbie's father, had doted on their son, spoiling him rotten. Maddy had set her sights on Robbie in junior high and pursued him relentlessly until he'd finally given in and asked her to the prom their senior year at Vineyard High School. They were together nearly every day after that, and before he went into the army, they'd found out she was pregnant. A quick trip to the Vineyard Justice of the Peace surprised both sets of parents, but they were young and too much in love to wait.

The memories of the night she'd found out Big Rob had died of a sudden heart attack a few weeks after Robbie was deployed to Afghanistan were still vivid in her mind. Since her husband had been unable to get back home to comfort his mother, she'd been left with the task and had done everything she could to ease Sandra's pain. Little did either woman know that less than six months later they'd be comforting each other over yet another death.

"Are you going to tell me or not?"

Maddy was jerked out of her walk down unpleasant memory lane and nodded. "Coffee's about ready. I guarantee both of us will need it." She meandered over to the pot and stood with her back to him to watch the dark liquid finish dripping. After filling two cups, she carried them back to where he sat. "I'm guessing you still take it black."

"Black and hot." He reached for it.

Sitting down next to him, she took a sip of the steaming liquid before she repeated the events of the horrible night.

"Jesus!" He jumped from his chair halfway through her rendition. "Some guy was in this house with a gun?"

"Yes," she said sadly. "I was hoping you'd seen something when you arrived that would prove he was really here."

"Why in the hell would you need to prove something like that?"

She finished the story, telling him how the phone and the text had disappeared, and how it came down to her word only. When her voice caught, he patted her hand.

"Maddy, no one could ever believe you had anything to do with killing Bernardi. What possible reason would you have to off that fat bastard?"

She shrugged before taking another sip of the hot coffee. "I don't know. Colt's at the hospital now talking to the guy who was in the cell next to Bernardi. Hopefully, he'll be able to shed some light on the situation."

"You didn't tell Colt I was at the diner, did you?" A look of panic spread across his face like a little boy who'd just done something naughty and hoped no one had noticed.

For the first time since Bernardi was killed, Maddy smiled. It was just like a man to worry about something like that only seconds after hearing about her traumatic experience. "Your secret's safe. No reason Colt needs to know about your quest to bed Miss Whatever-Her-Name-Is."

"Thank God for that!" A mischievous grin replaced the worried look. Holding up his thumb and forefinger, he said, "I'm this close to getting her between the sheets."

Why is getting laid the only thing the male species thinks about? The always hysterical Robin Williams got it right when he said that God gave men a brain and a penis, and only enough blood to run one at a time. Guess which one wins out every time?

Maddy choked on the sip of coffee and nearly spewed it across the table.

Tessa walked up and plopped her elbows down on the countertop. *Any news?*

"Colt's at the hospital now talking to the other guy," she answered her sister before remembering that Rogers had no idea Tessa was in the room.

She glanced his way, noticing his furrowed eyebrows. He must be wondering if she was going batty on him. She'd better get used to Tessa showing up whenever she pleased, or they'd be loading her onto the loony train before long. That's if they didn't put her in the paddy wagon first.

"I was just thinking we should dust Jessie's room for prints when she wakes up, although I have a feeling we won't find anything. Whoever planned this whole thing was pretty clever. I seriously doubt they'd be dumb enough to leave evidence." She hoped Rogers bought into her explanation for the surprised gasp.

"I agree. How do you think they got in?"

"If there're as smart as I think they are, they probably cased the joint and knew where Sandra hid the key."

Sheesh! That's inviting robbers to come on in and clean out the place. Hasn't anyone heard of keypads?

Maddy ignored Tessa and refilled Roger's cup. She was about to refill her own when she noticed Colt's police car pulling up to the curb outside. She ran to the front door and threw it open at the exact moment he walked up the steps onto the porch. One look at his face told her he was not bringing good news.

Her heart felt like it would beat out of her chest. "What did you find out, Colt?"

"I'm sorry, Maddy. I have to take you down to the station." He made eye contact with Rogers. "Stay here until I can send someone to relieve you. I don't want Jessie or her grandmother alone for a single minute."

"Why do I have to go to the station with you now?" Maddy asked, hoping he had a perfectly logical reason—one that didn't involve her wearing handcuffs.

His eyes clouded with sadness. "I talked with Alan Foxworthy before they wheeled him up to surgery. He fingered you as the shooter. I have no choice but to book you for Bernardi's murder."

Chapter Five

Jake Matthews nudged the dark-haired woman next to him in bed, but she didn't move. From the little he remembered about the night before, she'd already been two sheets of the proverbial three sheets to the wind when he'd picked her up at the hotel bar. He hadn't intended to bring her back to his room, but something about her had intrigued him.

Maybe because she could throw back a double bourbon better than he could. Or that she had more cleavage hanging out of the tight jersey knit dress than should have been legal.

He got out of bed and padded naked to the bathroom, catching a glimpse of himself in the mirror.

Jesus! When did he get the paunch? He'd worked hard for his six-pack abs, maintaining his as yet undefeated status as weight lifting champ at the Tri-City Police Olympics. Or at least since the last time he checked. Although he'd only been off the force a year now, he was definitely showing the consequences of neglecting his workout routine. When had all that flab snuck up on him? Apparently, the "use it or lose it" mantra was not just empty words.

Screw it!

He relieved himself, holding his head erect so the pounding was tolerable. Sneaking another look at his naked and not-so-buff physique, he grabbed his duffle bag from the floor and pulled out two extra strength aspirins before heading to the mini bar for something to swallow them with.

Halfway there, the woman in the bed let out the mother of all snores before rolling on her side, giving him an unrestricted view of her backside. Angela or Annie—some damn name with an A—had looked a whole lot sexier last night in the dim light of the bar. After getting that last glimpse of his naked self in the mirror moments before, he was sure she'd say the same thing about him. Alcohol had a way of masking the imperfections.

He stooped to open the minibar, causing his head to throb once again.

"Dammit!" he exclaimed as he stared into the unit.

He and Lady A had gone through every bottle of alcohol that had once occupied the first shelf. Desperate, he grabbed a Coke, popped it open, and swallowed the medicine, praying it would quickly work its magic.

Aware of the bad taste in his mouth, he chugged the rest of the soda. He hated that he was becoming more and more like his dad every day. Jake Senior would tie one on, then spend the next morning drinking God only knew how many soft drinks. When the vomiting began, followed by killer headaches, he'd curse the colas. It still amazed Jake that Senior never once considered that feeling like crap might have something to do with the fifth of Scotch he'd consumed the night before.

Jake and his younger brother Caleb would watch in anticipation, knowing how it would play out. The old man would start "cussing like a sailor" and his mother would scream at him for cursing in front of the children. He and Caleb would run and hide so Senior wouldn't hear them giggling, because there would've been hell to pay if he'd known they were laughing at him. Of course, there was always hell to pay for everything back then, and Jake still had the scars on his legs to prove it.

He would have to quit mixing his drinks and stick to good old draft beer. But he knew that wouldn't happen anytime soon. Beer never took him where the hard liquor did—never made him forget how he'd screwed up so many lives in a matter of minutes.

How he'd held his best friend in his arms as he took his last breath.

No, as bad as the after effects of hard drinking were, they didn't even come close to the pain he felt without it.

He jumped when the phone blared from the nightstand, grabbing another soda before heading that way to answer. He figured there was no hurry since Lady A was dead to the world and snoring like a lumberjack with her bare-naked ass in the air.

He grabbed the phone. "Yeah," he said into the receiver before easing down on the side of the bed.

He figured it was Tommy, the morning desk clerk, calling for some reason or another. He'd chosen this hotel because of its close proximity to both DFW airport and Vineyard, and he'd gotten friendly with several of the employees. Freddie, the night clerk, always made sure Jake made it from the bar to his room every night, and Tommy saw to it that no one disturbed him until noon every day.

He glanced at the alarm clock. Nine thirty. So why was Tommy calling him now?

"Jake?"

He straightened up, setting off another flurry of pounding above his right eye. "Why are you calling on the hotel phone?"

"Because you're not answering your other one. Is everything alright?"

Jake surveyed the area before spying his jeans in a heap across the room and his cell phone on the floor beside them. He'd probably turned off the ringer before he and Lady A had started celebrating.

"Battery's dead," he lied. "So what's up, boss?"

"There's been a new development in your case."

Jake popped the soda top and took a long swig, thinking he was never going to get rid of the feeling that he'd just gone through a West Texas dust storm with his mouth wide open. No wonder his dad had gulped down so many of the carbonated drinks the morning after. "What kind of new development?"

There was a long pause before the man on the other end cleared his throat. "He's dead."

Jake stood, turning once again to glance at the woman in the bed to make sure she was still asleep. He'd told her he was a computer software salesman in town for a convention. The last thing he needed was to complicate things. He had no plans of ever seeing her again, and the less she knew, the better.

He grabbed his jeans off the floor and scooped up the cell phone. Six missed calls. *Jesus!* He had to quit doing doubles.

"How did he die?" he asked, pulling the suitcase out of the closet, already anticipating the drive back home to San Antonio.

"They say a cop shot him in the Vineyard jail last night."

With the phone lodged between his ear and his neck, Jack stepped into his jeans and stopped halfway up his legs. "Why would a cop kill him?"

"We don't know, but it's time to go to Plan B. We need you to find out what the cop knows, and we need you to do it quickly."

So much for going back home. "I'm on it, boss," Jake said, shoving the suitcase back into the closet.

"Call as soon as you know something."

"Will do."

He hung up the phone and gave Lady A another gentle shove. It was obviously going to take more than a few shakes to wake her up, and right now, he didn't have the time or the patience to mess with it. He'd make sure Tommy sent up room service around noon. That's the least he could do for the woman after partying with her all night. It should have scared him that he couldn't remember if they'd had a good time, but it didn't. Right now he was more concerned with why the man he'd been tailing for the past two weeks had ended up dead in a jail cell.

Grabbing his car keys and cell phone, he exited the room and gently closed the door behind him, grinning at the absurdity of that. Not even a live heavy metal concert in the room would wake up the buxom brunette.

On the first floor, he stopped and made the arrangements with Tommy to take care of Lady A, then walked out into the cold November Texas air. On the fifteen minute ride to Vineyard, he'd already begun racking his brain for a reason why a cop would want to kill a prisoner under his watch. He'd had eyes on the guy as late as ten the night before, but he'd left the Vineyard bar right after the cops had hauled the mark's sorry ass to jail. Seems Gino Bernardi had gotten jealous when another drunk made some kind of remark about his girlfriend, and he'd pounded the guy.

Figuring Bernardi's lawyer would play the get-out-of-jail-free card and have him home before most people had consumed their first cup of coffee, Jake had headed back to the hotel to celebrate the rest of Thanksgiving in his own way.

The whole thing made no sense—at least not yet. But he hadn't been a cop for over ten years without learning that *nothing* was ever coincidental.

There was a reason behind the killing, and he was being paid good money to find out if that reason involved a piece of jewelry.

* * * * *

Maddy sat at her desk watching the police station come alive with activity. Although she'd been fingerprinted and booked,

Colt hadn't insisted she sit in a cell while she waited for Lainey to come through with the name of a good criminal lawyer.

She shuddered at the thought that she even needed a lawyer much less a criminal defense attorney. Lainey worked in downtown Dallas as the weekend anchor on the six o'clock news for a local station, and although she didn't know any defense lawyers personally, she had access to people who did. She'd been on the phone to her colleagues ever since she'd come to the station an hour ago.

Maddy blew out a breath, hoping somehow this would all magically go away, but she knew that was wishful thinking. Even though right now she was on leave *with* pay, she wasn't sure her financial situation could handle too much time off. Things would go south in a hurry if a grand jury thought there was enough evidence to go forward with a murder charge. She was already counting every penny as it was, and just last week at the grocery store, she'd had to put back a couple of items she'd decided they could live without.

It wouldn't kill her and Jessie if they didn't eat ice cream or cookies while she got her savings back on track. She might even lose a few of those unwanted pounds she'd packed on in the past few months. Eating healthy wasn't cheap, another casualty of her money crisis.

"Maddy, I think I found someone."

She glanced up at Lainey, noticing how pretty her sister was even this early in the morning. Of all the siblings, Lainey looked the most like Tessa, who had been–hands down—the best looking of the bunch. She decided to keep that observation to herself for now. Despite the fact that Lainey and Tessa had ended their nine-year estrangement the year before, Lainey was still uncomfortable when people mentioned the resemblance. Tessa had used her looks to get what she wanted in the world and hadn't been above screwing anyone who stood in her way. Lainey wanted no part of even the slightest comparison.

Maddy reached for the slip of paper in her sister's hand. "Joseph Newland of Newland, Rhodes, and Associates," she read aloud. "They sound expensive."

"Seriously, Maddy? You're going to go bargain hunting when there's a possibility you might have to spend the rest of your life in jail for a murder you didn't commit?" Lainey scolded, before she softened and moved closer. Bending down, she hugged her sister. "I've been told this guy is the best. Besides, that's what families are for. Tessa left me the vineyard when she died, and Deena and Kate will want to pitch in, too."

Maddy gave a fake laugh. "The vineyard burned down, remember? I've heard you say too many times that what little income you're getting from selling wine made with someone else's grapes is only enough to cover operating costs while you wait for the new vines to produce. And Deena has to answer to that jackass husband of hers for every penny she spends."

Lainey opened her mouth to argue, but Maddy silenced her with her hand. "Then there's Kate who eats every meal away from the hospital at my house because her paycheck as an obstetrical resident is so pathetic. And God knows I can't afford another payment." She shook her head. "I'm sure there are cheaper—"

"Hush," Lainey interrupted. "We'll find a way. I've already lost one sister, and I'm not about to lose another because we used a discount lawyer." She grabbed the slip of paper back from Maddy and pulled out her cell phone.

Maddy listened to her leave a message with the lawyer's answering service. She'd forgotten this was Thanksgiving and most people had taken the long weekend off. Obviously Newland and Rhodes were enjoying the mini vacation, too.

It didn't seem possible that less than twenty-four hours earlier, they'd all been sitting around Deena's dining room table giving thanks and enjoying each other's company. The only thing she'd worried about then was how many miles she'd have to jog around her neighborhood to burn off all the calories from her sister's phenomenal desserts.

At the thought of the Thanksgiving feast, Maddy remembered that Deena had sent a piece of pumpkin pie crunch and a bowl of ambrosia to the station, her favorites. She'd been just about to snack on them when she'd gotten the phone call, and all hell had broken loose.

She looked around for the insulated lunch carrier Deena had used. Not seeing it anywhere, she assumed Colt had put it back into the refrigerator in the break room. She made a mental note to make sure it got back to Deena before one of the guys snagged it.

"What do we do now?" she asked, feeling the hope slide from her body. If they couldn't get a lawyer to facilitate her release on bail, she'd have to spend the next three days in a jail cell. Feeling a tear slide down her cheek, she turned away and dabbed at it, hoping Lainey hadn't seen. As the oldest sister of the clan, she'd always had to be the strong one for her younger siblings in the one-parent household.

Her mother had done the best she could after their father had died when Maddy was not yet in her teens. He'd stopped to help a stranded motorist and was killed by a drunken driver who'd later confessed he thought he'd hit a deer. The man's license had been revoked two months before the accident for a second DUI, and he didn't even have the collision insurance required for all Texas drivers.

With only the minimal life insurance they'd used to bury him, the family had received no other compensation, and Sylvia Garcia had been forced to work two jobs just to make ends meet. At the tender age of fifteen, Maddy had grown up quickly, giving up a lot of high school activities to care for her younger siblings. It pained her that now she was the one needing their help.

Just then the front door pushed open and Kate and Deena rushed in, running directly to Maddy and encircling her in a group hug.

"Oh my God! How could anyone think you killed someone?" Deena asked, unable to stop the tears making a path down her cheeks. She and Maddy had always been best friends growing up and were still close. "What's gonna happen to you now?"

Maddy pulled away from her sisters when she noticed that Tessa had returned and had flopped down ungracefully on the edge of the desk.

She turned to the others. "Can any of you see her?"

"See who?" Kate asked before slapping her head. "Don't tell me Tessa's here. I thought she went off into the light after we found out who killed her."

Tessa laughed. *Kate has always been the smartass and the most like me of any of you. That's why I adore her.* She put her finger to her forehead and saluted the youngest Garcia sister. *Tell her the light gave me a migraine, and I'm back.*

"She showed up right before Bernardi was killed," Maddy explained. "Somehow, she knew I was about to get into trouble, and she came back to help."

"So she's like our guardian angel now?" Deena asked, moving behind her older sister. Tessa had always intimidated her, and even dead, she, apparently, had the same effect.

Something like that, Tessa said, now filing her nail. *God knows Deena needs looking after with that limp dick of a husband she lives with.*

"She said yes, she's our new guardian angel. And she's been sent back to help me," Maddy said before giggling. "That and the fact that she's up to her old flirty ways up there and managed to piss off the Gatekeeper's wife." She pointed to the ceiling.

"Ha! I would've thought she was giving old Lucifer a run for his money. Showing him what hot really meant, or at the very least, planning a fund raiser to pay for air conditioning down there," Kate said, a mischievous glint lighting her eyes.

Kate had better watch out. With that mouth of hers, the good people of Vineyard will start calling her a mini me if she's not careful. Although Tessa tried to sound stern, the sparkle in her eyes told an entirely different story. It was as if she were proud that her baby sister was perfecting that sarcastic wit and following in her footsteps.

They all turned when the door to Colt's office opened and he walked out, his face etched with worry.

"Did you find a lawyer?" he asked Lainey.

"I have the name of a well known attorney from Dallas with a good track record in murder trials, but I had to leave a message with his answering service. They said he won't be back in the office until Monday, and they'd give him the message."

Colt focused his attention back on Maddy. "Not much going on down at the courthouse today, but I just talked to Judge Reynolds. He's scheduled your arraignment hearing for this afternoon."

"What if we don't hear from the Dallas lawyer by then?" Maddy asked, the fear slipping back into her voice.

"Already taken care of. I called Charlie Prescott and asked him to appear with you so we can get you released on bail."

That SOB. He tried to screw me over, Tessa shouted.

Maddy rephrased Tessa's comment. "Do you trust him after what he almost did to Tessa?"

"No, but we're kinda in a bind here. No one's going to come downtown today and represent you, knowing they'll be fired as soon as a better lawyer comes along." He paused. "Charlie's walked the straight and narrow ever since he tried to work a double deal and get Lainey to sell the vineyard after Tessa died. Besides, he owes me for not locking him up in jail over that." He looked around the room. "Is Tessa here now?"

Maddy nodded and pointed to the edge of the desk.

"Tell her not to interfere with this investigation." He turned to the other Garcia sisters. "That goes for all of you as well. Whoever killed the prisoner wasn't just some local hothead who thought Bernardi might have gotten too friendly with his woman last night. If what I suspect is true, this was a well-planned, perfectly executed hit, and there aren't too many people in the area capable of pulling off something like that. You ladies are liable to screw up any chance this department has of clearing Maddy. Or worse, get yourselves killed if you go running around town asking too many questions like you did when Tessa died." He turned to his wife. "Need I remind you, Lainey, that you nearly burned up with the grapevines because you got too close?"

"Colt?"

He whirled around to face Danny Landers, who had just walked up and looked like he was about to cry.

"I think you'd better have a look at this."

Colt snatched the faxed report from his deputy's hand and quickly read it without changing his facial expression.

Maddy tried to get Danny's attention to see if she could get some hint about the report, but the young officer kept his eyes riveted to the floor.

Oh, boy! This isn't going to be good, she thought. Danny was the prankster of the group and always had a devilish look in his eyes. He was like a younger brother to her, and if he couldn't even make eye contact with her now, whatever was in that report had to be really bad.

Even Tessa sat speechless, waiting to find out what the document held. That, in itself, was not a good sign. She tended to joke about everything.

Finally, Colt looked up, and his face showed the concern. He headed straight to Maddy's desk. "Where did you get twenty-five grand last week?"

"What? I haven't seen that much money all at one time in—well, forever." Her heart felt like it had stopped beating. Why would Colt ask a question like that?

He laid the report in front of her. "Then how do you explain this?"

She reached for it, praying it didn't really say what she suspected from Colt's questions. But today was not going to be her day for having prayers answered. Glancing at her bank statement, she let her eyes linger on the twenty-five thousand dollar deposit made two days ago. She tried to say something—to deny it—but nothing came out. All she could do was stare at the horrified look on her sisters' faces as they stood by helplessly.

In a matter of a few minutes, her situation had gone from bad to catastrophic. Right in front of her was proof that someone was trying to frame her. This would make her story about why she allowed a killer to walk into the station and murder a prisoner in cold blood on her watch suspect.

And worse—now they had motive.

Chapter Six

"This is worse than I thought," Colt said, reaching for the report that could be the smoking gun to send his sister-in-law to jail. "If someone has gone to all this trouble to deposit money in your bank account, Maddy, we're not talking small time here. This is beginning to smell like organized crime." He turned to Danny Landers. "Run over to Vineyard National Bank and get a look at the security tapes for the day before Thanksgiving. Call me the minute you know something."

Landers patted Maddy's back and attempted a smile before he charged off with the bank information in hand.

Colt turned to the three sisters who had yet to say a word. "You three need to let me do my job and figure this all out. I mean it." He zeroed in on Maddy. "And I will figure it out. I promise." Narrowing his eyes, he shot a warning look in his wife's direction. "If I find out any of you questioned even one person about this or stuck your nose in my investigation in any way, I swear I'll lock you all up." He swiveled around and charged back into his office, mumbling under his breath.

Maddy glanced first at Lainey, then at Deena and Kate before settling on Tessa, whose eyes were now lit up with mischief.

Yeah! Like that's gonna happen!

For some reason, hearing her sister say what she'd been thinking gave her a twinge of hope, and for the first time since she'd arrived at the station, Maddy smiled.

"Okay, we have to get going on this," Lainey said, looking up at the clock on the wall over Lander's empty desk. She stole a glance over her shoulder to make sure Colt wasn't watching before leaning in and lowering her voice. "Let's meet up in an hour to figure out how we're going to do it."

"We can use my place," Deena said, huddling closer. "Mike's running around town catching up on business this morning, so we'll have the whole house to ourselves."

Well I'll be damned. My sisters have all grown balls. I couldn't be prouder at this moment. Tessa's gaze moved from one sibling to another.

"One o'clock at my house," Deena said. "I'll have a pitcher of margaritas ready and waiting."

* * * * *

He rolled off her body and took several slow deep breaths. *Damn!* The woman was a workout, but worth every ounce of energy he expended.

"Do you want to go again?"

He turned to her, unbelieving. There was no way he could go another round—at least not without drugs. "Darling, as much as I'd love to show you again why I keep you around, that isn't going to be physically possible for awhile." He reached over and kissed her neck. "Give me a few hours, and then we'll talk."

She nuzzled closer, spooning his body with hers, and he cringed. This was the part he hated. If he had his way, she'd go to one of the guest rooms until he summoned her back for more play time. He never could understand why women felt the need to touch after sex. He was about to suggest that they'd both get more sleep if they were in separate beds when he felt her hand inching its way around his back to his abdomen.

God! The woman was insatiable.

He knew that despite his lack of interest at the moment, she'd work magic with those hands of hers, and before too much longer, they'd be having wild monkey sex again. As awesome as that sounded, right now he needed sleep.

Turning over, he pulled her closer, virtually stopping her fingers from finding their mark. "Did I tell you what a fantastic job you did last night, lover?" he asked, thinking if he could get her talking, he might be able to be on his way to that much needed rest.

When they'd finally made it back home last night, both were on a high and giddy about what they'd just done, and after the cocaine and the Johnnie Walker Red, they'd partied all night long. He wondered why she wasn't as strung out as he was.

"Why don't you show me how much you appreciate me?" she purred.

Okay, that little ploy obviously hadn't worked.

He ran his hands through her long red hair, thinking it was those curls that had first attracted him to her a few months ago. Although he usually went for brunettes, something about her had caught his attention immediately. He grinned to himself, thinking that *something* probably was the double D's threatening to spill out of the black silk halter top she'd worn the night he'd spotted her from across the bar.

"You know that diamond bracelet you fell in love with when we were shopping at the Galleria last week?"

Her eyes lit up and she nodded.

"Well, I think you earned it."

When she squealed with delight, he mentally high-fived himself for distracting her. The woman loved jewelry and would do just about anything to get it. The clever part was that he'd already planned on buying it for her anyway. The demand for drugs had escalated the past few months, and he had quite a nice stash of extra cash on hand. Now he could use it as the perfect opportunity to get her mind off more sex.

Before he could suggest they swallow a downer and catch a little shuteye, his cell phone began to vibrate on the nightstand.

Reaching for it, he saw his mother's picture pop up on caller ID, and he slid out of bed. "Got to take this, doll," he said over his shoulder as he padded naked into the bathroom. He locked the door behind him and answered. "Hey, Mom, what's going on?"

He'd taken her to the Regency Hotel yesterday for a Thanksgiving buffet and hadn't been able to get away quickly enough. He loved his mother, but nothing he ever did pleased her. She spent nearly every waking minute crying these days.

Before she even said a word, he heard her sniffle, and a ball of fire erupted in his abdomen.

"I can't sleep anymore," she sobbed. "Everywhere I look I see Junior calling out to me for help."

He swallowed hard. "Mama, I told you, Junior probably hightailed it to Mexico because the cops were about to arrest him again. Remember?"

"Why didn't he tell me goodbye before he left? Why doesn't he call to tell me he's okay? I'm really worried something is terribly wrong this time."

"I don't know why he doesn't call, Mama. You know how he disappears for days without calling and then just shows up like nothing's wrong. That's the way he is."

"He's got to know how worried I am. I love him more than anything else in this world, and now I'm all alone."

No matter how many times he told himself she didn't mean that, it still hurt to hear her say that, as if he meant nothing to her. If only once she would look at him like he was worth something. She had two sons, dammit! And although he knew exactly why Junior had disappeared, he wasn't about to tell his mother. It would kill her, and she would never speak to him again.

The truth was he'd spent his entire life getting his older brother out of trouble of some form or another. He'd overlooked the many thousands of dollars of his product that had ended up his brother's nose or injected into his veins, but his latest screw-up had been too bad to look the other way.

He drew the line when it came to messing with his business. He'd worked too hard to get where he was today.

He closed his eyes, remembering his brother's lifeless eyes three weeks ago. Instead of remorse, he only felt anger that Junior was still causing him trouble, even from his watery grave.

After comforting his mother for a few more minutes, he managed to calm her down before hanging up. But he knew in his heart that no matter what he said or did, no matter how much money he spent trying to make her feel better, his mother would never get over the fact that her oldest son was no longer around. She'd never feel even half the love for him despite the fact that he was the one paying all her bills and caring for her.

He opened the medicine cabinet and pulled out the plastic bag hidden inside a hollowed out can of deodorant. After spreading the white powder on the counter, he snorted first one line, then another. Then he allowed his gaze to linger on the man in the mirror. How could someone with his kind of power and money be so helpless when it came to fixing the situation with his own mother?

"I had to do it, Junior," he said aloud before wiping a small amount of white residue from his nose and walking back into the bedroom.

He couldn't think about his mother or his brother now. The drugs had made him horny as hell again.

Sliding the sheet back, he climbed in beside the woman who was watching him with a confused look on her face. "Spread your legs, sweetheart. I'm going to make you sing."

* * * * *

Maddy stopped to pick up chips and salsa from Taco Loco on the way to her sister's. Deena would have tons of sweet stuff left over from the Thanksgiving meal the day before, but they needed salty treats to go with her sister's famous margarita swirls. She arrived a few minutes late, and everyone was already there—everyone, that is, except Tessa. She wondered if her younger sister had flaked out once again and returned to wherever ghosts go when they're not scaring people.

Deena met her at the front door with a bear hug. "Yum. These can be our first course before we get to the leftover desserts from yesterday. Good thing I made guacamole." She pulled her sister inside the house. "Come on. Lainey and Kate have already started working on a list of things we need to do."

Now that's scary all by itself. The two braniac Garcia girls matching wits. Bet they've already solved the murder.

Maddy smiled at Tessa, who was now leading the way into the kitchen. God help her, but somehow, knowing she had come from somewhere up above gave her a warm feeling, as if the big Man up there had sent His own personal help.

Okay, so far she hadn't been very helpful, but Maddy still held out hope. Before Tessa died, she'd been a prominent figure in Vineyard's high society club. She knew things about some of the locals that even Maddy and the police department weren't privy to.

Both Kate and Lainey jumped up to greet her when she walked in.

"We're going to find the SOB who's trying to frame you, sis. Promise," Kate said. "But first, we need carbs." She grabbed the chips out of Maddy's hand. "This should do it. Chips from Taco Loco are the best."

"Here." Deena handed Maddy a frozen margarita swirl. "You need to drink up, kiddo. You're already two behind the rest of us."

Maddy took a sip and smacked her lips. The frozen lime concoction was made exactly the way she liked it with just the right amount of tequila and triple sec. The sangria wine swirled into it made it taste more like a high calorie dessert than an alcoholic beverage. She took another big drink and immediately got brain freeze. "Whoa! I'd forgotten that you can't drink these fast."

"Sit here," Kate said, sliding a chair next to hers. "Lainey and I listed all the people who might want to see something bad happen to you."

Maddy was about to take another long swallow and stopped halfway to her mouth. "Do you really think someone has a personal vendetta against me or that I was just the perfect patsy?" She reached for the list and tsked when she saw the first entry. "Why would Darrell Livingston want to hurt me?"

"Oh, I don't know. Maybe because you humiliated him at church a few weeks back when he asked you out on a date in front of the entire congregation," Lainey said. "You don't remember how pissed off he was when you turned him down flat?"

"You can't be serious, Lainey. Half the women at church have turned him down."

Definitely patsy, Tessa said. *If someone hated you enough to ruin your life, it would have been easier to just kill Jessie when they had the opportunity.*

The reminder about how close her daughter had come to being hurt—or worse—caused Maddy to close her eyes and suck in a big gulp of air before responding. "You're probably right, Tessa. As a rookie cop they must've known I'd be vulnerable."

"She's here, again?" Deena asked, moving a little closer to Maddy. "And what's she right about this time?"

"She thinks if someone really wanted to hurt me, they would have..." She swallowed hard trying to repeat what Tessa has said. "Done something to Jessie," she finally blurted, unable to make herself say the word killed.

"Good thinking, sis. Death becomes you," Kate said with a glint in her eye.

Tessa threw back her head and laughed out loud. *Christ, that girl has a mouth on her.*

"Okay, so let's start with that assumption and go from there," Lainey said. "If they weren't looking to hurt you, Maddy, their goal must've been to kill Gino Bernardi or the other guy in the cell next to him. What do we know about either of them?"

Maddy turned to Tessa who shrugged. She'd get no help there.

I know just about everyone in the county, especially the men, and I've never heard his name before. He must be new to Vineyard.

Kate pulled out her iPad and Googled him. When nothing came up, she looked confused. "Everybody has at least one or two hits when you Google their name. Let me try this again." After the second attempt produced the same results, she shook her head. "And now we have our first mystery. Why does a man like Bernardi not have a history?"

"That's a good place to start," Maddy said. "I won't be allowed access to the police files, but I'm pretty sure I can talk Tom Rogers into helping us on the side." She turned to her younger sister. "And you can work on getting Danny Landers to share some information every now and then. He's had the hots for you since junior high. Think you can warm him up a little and get him in the mood to help?"

"Me? I'm already in a relationship, remember? What do you think I can do, anyhow?"

"For starters, just be nice to him."

And wear that red and blue blouse of yours that shows off your cleavage.

"Great idea," Maddy said, before she remembered she was the only one who could hear Tessa. "Your sister said to remind you not to leave the house without that sexy red blouse when you go to talk to him."

"I am not sleeping with him," Kate said, emphatically. "I'm not that kind a girl."

Everyone's that kind of girl, Tessa said. *Some do it for money, others for the power, and you, little sister, need to do it to save your big sister's ass.*

Maddy swiveled in her chair to face Kate. "No one's asking you to sleep with him, Katie. Just be nice." She paused and winked. "And what would it hurt to show him a little skin while you're at it? He can be a valuable asset to us."

Kate blew out a breath before the beginning of a smile tipped her lips. "It might be nice to get out of those ugly scrubs for a change." She high-fived Maddy. "I'll do it. The poor boy won't know what hit him when I'm done with him."

"Perfect," Lainey said. "You work on Danny to get the police files on Bernardi, and we'll go from there." She turned to Maddy. "Didn't you say Bernardi ended up in jail because the other guy made a pass at his girlfriend?" When Maddy nodded, she continued. "We need to find out her name and pay her a visit. If anyone knows who might have it out for Bernardi, it'll be her."

"I'll get Rogers working on that," Maddy said.

"Okay then," Deena said. "Now that we have a plan, who wants leftover Pumpkin Pie Crunch?"

When they all raised their hands, Deena got up and walked over to the counter to dish out the dessert. For a few minutes after she placed the plates in front of her sisters, there was silence in the kitchen. The cold hard fact that Maddy had a murder charge hanging over her head was forgotten as they devoured the rich dessert.

God, I love her Pumpkin Pie Crunch, Tessa said. *It sucks being dead.*

Maddy was about to tell her how much they all missed her when her cell phone blared, and she nearly jumped out of her chair. After taking a quick swallow of her margarita to wash down the last bite of the dessert, she answered, "Hello."

"Is this Madelyn Castillo?"

"Yes. Who's this?" The voice was low and sexy and not one she recognized.

"Anthony Pirelli," the man responded. "I heard about your arrest for the murder of a prisoner in your custody, and I'd like to offer representation."

Maddy shot up in the chair, her eyes wide now. "Who did you say you were?" She mouthed the word *lawyer* to her sisters who were all huddled close by now, hanging on to her every word.

"Anthony Pirelli of Pirelli and Associates. We're located in the Shaffer Building in downtown Dallas. Let me explain why I'm calling." He paused as if to give her time to take it all in. "I received a phone call from a colleague about your case. He convinced me that you have been unjustly accused and that I could be of some help in clearing your name."

"Why would you want to represent me, Mr. Pirelli?" Maddy interrupted, putting special emphasis on his name for Lainey who had already opened up her iPad and was now doing a Google search of his name.

"If you do your homework on me, you'll find that I have a ninety percent success rate in criminal court. I do have an ulterior motive, though. There's no question this case will generate national news coverage. I'd like to be standing beside you when it does. I've already taken the liberty of speaking with a Sheriff Winslow at the Vineyard Police Station who brought me up to speed on the preliminary facts about your case. Unfortunately—"

"I'm afraid there's no way I can afford you," Maddy said, after Lainey looked up from viewing his webpage and mouthed *Big bucks*. She felt the hope drain from her body. Her worst nightmare was having Charlie Prescott representing her, but it looked like she might not have a choice in the matter.

"You didn't let me finish, Ms. Castillo," he said, unable to keep the annoyance out of his voice. "What I was about to say is that I can't make it out to Vineyard today because of a prior commitment, but Sheriff Winslow has assured me that a local attorney will stand in for the arraignment hearing. The sheriff sees no reason why this other lawyer won't be successful in getting a reasonable bail set. The purpose of my call today is to set up a time on Monday to come out to Vineyard and sit down with you to discuss how we're going to proceed. That's if you'll hire me."

Maddy gasped. "You're willing to defend me?"

For the first time since he'd called, the man chuckled. "I wouldn't have called if I wasn't. I don't have to solicit business, Ms. Castillo. My practice speaks for itself. So can we meet Monday morning at your house to discuss this?"

A horrible thought pulsed through her, and she forced herself to say it out loud. "I'm afraid you might want to reconsider before making that long drive, Mr. Pirelli. As I said, there's no way I can come up with enough money to cover your fees."

"Why don't you let me worry about that. As I said, I have a stake in this, too. So, shall we say eleven on Monday then?"

A tear slid down Maddy's cheek. "Eleven's good. I look forward to meeting you," she said before hanging up the phone and dropping her head into her hands.

Help was on the way—and not just any help. Lainey had pulled up several articles in the NY Times and several other prestigious magazines listing Pirelli as one of the top criminal defense lawyers in the Metroplex. That alone was enough to lift Maddy's spirits.

She glanced up at her sisters who were all staring, anxiously waiting to hear what he'd said. "I don't know how I'll pay this man, but I'm convinced I no longer have a choice. Whatever I have to do to come up with the money, I'll do. He's my only hope." She reached for her drink and chugged it, deciding it was well worth the painful brain freeze.

If she was going to be there to guide Jessie through her turbulent teenage years, her best chance was driving up from Dallas on Monday to talk to her about how they would make that happen. Now all she had to do was find a way to pay him.

Chapter Seven

The next day Maddy appeared alongside Charlie Prescott in front of the county judge who turned out to be a guy she'd dated in high school. After asking about his wife and kids, she'd stood silently next to Charlie as he petitioned for a ridiculously low bail. Several minutes later she'd walked out of the courtroom after Charlie himself paid the twenty thousand dollar bond. She figured Tessa's old lawyer was still trying to get back on the sheriff's good side after nearly screwing Colt's only daughter Gracie out of Tessa's inheritance.

She spent all day Sunday home alone with Jessie, trying hard not to think about how it had only taken a short period of time for her life to get completely messed up. They'd ordered pizza and watched a rerun of The Sound of Music, Jessie's favorite movie. For twenty-four hours, she'd managed to stay positive about everything, but as soon as she'd awakened on Monday, the feeling of impending doom and gloom had returned with a vengeance.

When Tom Rogers showed up with Bernardi's police records, she grabbed his arm, pulled him into the house, and slammed the door.

"No one followed you here, did they?" she asked, worried that her brother-in-law had somehow found out about her plan to get information from her colleague.

Although he shook his head, his eyes darted back and forth as if he half expected his boss to suddenly appear and chew him out. "Colt can't ever know I'm giving you this."

Maddy grabbed the arrest report out of his hand. "Why would I tell him and screw up my only chance of keeping up with the investigation? Since I'm not allowed anywhere near the station I need you as my inside guy."

He studied her face a few minutes before nodding. "You've got a point. But Colt made it perfectly clear to all of us this morning that no information about your case is to be leaked to anyone, especially not the press."

"Do I look like the press to you?"

"No," he answered quickly. "But your name was the next one out of Colt's mouth with the no-information warning."

She narrowed her eyes. "He actually said no one could tell me anything about the case?"

"Yep, and he'd kick my butt all the way to Dallas if he knew I was here right now." He glanced out the window. "He's probably got someone on my tail already."

Maddy couldn't help but laugh. Rogers was affectionately known as the king of paranoia at the precinct, the one most likely to come face-to-face with the boogeyman one day.

"He won't find out," she reassured him. "Unless you open your big mouth. Now sit down and tell me what you know so far." She motioned toward the kitchen. "Want coffee?"

"No thanks. I had three cups at the diner before breakfast and several more at the station."

"Oh yeah, I forgot about your little mission to get laid, diner waitress style."

He grinned, and for a moment Maddy was sure he had scored a touchdown in that department.

"I'm closer, but she's harder to crack than I thought." He plopped down on the couch, sending one of the throw pillows to the floor. "I gotta make this quick so Colt doesn't come driving down the street and see my black and white parked out front."

She picked up the pillow and threw it to the other side of the couch. "Okay then, let's hear it."

He pointed his finger at her. "I'm telling you right now, Maddy, something fishy was going on with Bernardi."

Tell us something we don't know, moron, Tessa said, suddenly appearing and sitting down beside him.

Maddy was sure the pillow would end up on the floor once again and she was already formulating a lie to explain it to Rogers.

But it never moved.

Tessa surveyed the cop next to her before turning back to Maddy. *Please tell me you never did him.*

"God, no," Maddy said before she could stop herself. She snuck a peek Rogers's way and found him looking at her as if she were talking to a ghost, which only made her laugh out loud at the irony. "I meant that's all we needed. The case is jacked up enough without adding new strange stuff. We all know that Bernardi was a jerk, but what do you mean something was fishy, Tom?"

He leaned forward, lowering his voice. "All we can find out about him is that he moved to Vineyard a little over three months ago, and other than his girlfriend, he really hasn't made friends with anyone else in town."

"I'll admit that's unusual, but a lot of people who move to a new town never take the time to find a group of friends they're comfortable with. He may have known he wouldn't be around long and didn't bother." She bit her lower lip, something she always did when she was concentrating on something. "So what about his workplace? No friends there, either?"

"He works out of his house."

"Doing what?" she asked.

"This is where it gets really weird." Tessa moved close enough to him that he should have smelled her breath, if ghosts even had smells, but he didn't have a clue that she was practically on top of him now. "He does the payroll for a couple of small businesses in Vineyard."

"And why is that weird?"

"I'm guessing he makes even less money than you and me," he said, pushing his butt into the back of the couch.

Maddy threw her hands in the air. She was getting frustrated with the conversation. "Come on, Tom, get to the point. I have an appointment at eleven."

"Okay, okay. Here's the thing. The guy was wearing a Rolex watch the night we arrested him. Do you know anybody making our kind of money walking around in one of those?"

She thought about it. "No, but it still doesn't seem all that strange to me. Could've been a gift or part of an inheritance. Or he could have boosted it from some dumb rich guy."

"So how do you account for the five thousand bucks he had in his pocket?"

That got her attention. "He had five grand on him at the bar?" She whistled. "Who carries that kinda cash around?"

He slapped his knee. "That's what I'm saying, Maddy. Something's fishy." He glanced down at his own watch before springing up from the couch. "Gotta go. I told Colt I'd swing by Cowboys Galore and have a chat with the bartender."

"Let me go with you," she pleaded, thinking if she could just get one lead from the place where Bernardi and the other guy had been arrested that night, she and her sisters could start checking things out on their own. Maybe the bartender would remember some little thing that might help. "I'll stay in the background and won't say a word. I promise."

"Thought you said you had an appointment or something. It's already ten forty-five and I can't wait."

She grabbed his arm. "Please, please, please, Tom. You owe me for not telling Colt why I was the only one at the station for so long the night Bernardi was killed." She hated having to use that against him. "Besides my appointment will be over by noon. You have to wait and let me go with you, or I'll go crazy sitting here by myself. You can tell Colt the guy wasn't in until later."

"Christ, Maddy. You're going to get me fired yet." He headed for the door before turning back. "Okay, I'll grab some lunch and come back for you around one thirty, but you can't ride in the squad car with me."

"That'll work," she said, blowing him a kiss. "I should be done by then, and I'll be waiting for you."

After he climbed into his car and pulled away from her driveway, she clapped her hands in glee. Finally, she'd be able to do something besides sit around the house feeling sorry for herself.

Make a list of questions we need to ask the bartender, Tessa said. *We have to be prepared.*

"You're coming with me?"

Her sister tsked. *Who knows how to get a bartender to talk better than me? But first I want to get a look at this hotshot lawyer coming from Dallas.* She sighed. *Too bad I'm dead. If I could have only one night with him, you wouldn't have to worry about how you're going to come up with the cash. He'd be begging to take the case gratis.*

Maddy smirked. "Even dead, you're still pretty cocky."

Hey! When you got it... She paused when the doorbell rang, a sparkle suddenly flashing in her eyes. *Here we go, Maddy. We're about to eyeball the Italian dude who's gonna keep your pretty little ass out of jail.*

After sneaking a peek into the mirror on the way to the door, Maddy took a deep breath. *Crap!* She cursed the fact that she didn't have time to put on a little lipstick or at least to re-comb her hair, then decided she was an idiot. The man standing outside her door right now was going to try to keep her out of jail, not take her to the prom.

As soon as she got her first look at him, she added a few more mental curse words for not slapping on some makeup.

Holy guacamole! I think I've died and gone to heaven, Tessa said before chuckling. *Oh wait, been there—done that. But I can assure you, big sister, there's no one up there that looks like him.*

"Ms. Castillo?"

Maddy could only nod and pray that her mouth wasn't hanging open. She'd seen a lot of good looking men in her life but only a few who qualified as beautiful. Anthony Pirelli was in that small percentile.

"May I come in?"

She was acting like a teenage girl with an up-close look at a rock star instead of a woman meeting her defense lawyer for the first time. She attempted a smile. "Pardon my manners. I just wasn't expecting someone so"—she searched for the right word—"young."

His eyes crinkled. "That's what most of the DAs say when they first meet me. It gives me an instant advantage since they associate young with inexperienced." He walked through the doorway. "But it doesn't take them long to realize looks mean absolutely nothing in a courtroom, Ms. Castillo. And for the record, I'm thirty-two."

"Call me Maddy," she said, walking around him to face him when he stopped in the middle of her living room. "Do you want to work in here or at the kitchen table, Mr. Pirelli?"

"If I'm going to call you Maddy, then you'll need to drop the Mr. Pirelli. It's Tony. I can assure you we're going to get very personal before this is over." He pointed to the kitchen. "Let's go in there. It will be easier if I have a flat surface to work on."

Something about the way those words rolled off his tongue brought images of just what they could do on a flat surface before she mentally scolded herself. The man had said personal, not intimate. She needed to get her thoughts out of the bedroom.

She led the way and motioned for him to have a seat at the table. "Would you like a cup of coffee, Tony?"

He laid his briefcase on the table and then sat down. "I'd love some. Just a little cream, please."

Turning her back to him, she brewed a new pot, wishing she had some of Deena's phenom baking skills. What she wouldn't give to impress this man with a coffee cake made from scratch or one of the other rich desserts her sister was famous for.

After she poured two cups, she walked to the table and sat down opposite him. Sliding one his way, she said. "Where do you want to start?"

"First off, can I assume everything went well at the arraignment on Saturday?"

She nodded. "I was back home in less than an hour."

"Good. So how about if you tell me in your own words exactly what happened the night Gino Bernardi was killed."

Check the clock, Maddy. Don't you watch The Good Wife? Time with a lawyer is similar to putting a frozen dinner in the microwave. Although it only takes five minutes, you're billed like it'd been cooking for hours. You'd better get the money part out of the way before you go any further.

For once, she agreed with her dead sister. "First, I think we need to talk about your fee. I'm not a wealthy woman with a lot of cash at my fingertips, so I need to plan ahead." She gulped, wishing she didn't have to ask. "How much are we talking about here?"

He held her captive with his eyes for a few minutes, sending an involuntary shiver up her arms. "Depends on how long it takes and how much time and money are necessary for discovery."

"A guesstimate?" She broke the eye contact and blew out a breath, hoping his response wouldn't crush her excitement.

"As I mentioned on the phone the other day, I'm representing you at a reduced rate—actually at less than a third of my usual fee—for two reasons. As soon as my colleague called to suggest I take this case, I did some research into the circumstances of Bernardi's death. My initial gut instinct was that something wasn't right about this whole thing. Regardless of whether you did it or not, I wanted the opportunity to be involved."

"And the second reason?"

He leaned back in the chair and folded his hands behind his head, again nailing her with a stare. "I'm not a saint, Maddy. Like I said in the beginning, this is one of those high-profile cases that will be all over the news. One day I hope to enter politics, and the exposure can't hurt."

There it is! His all-about-himself motive. For a minute I was beginning to believe maybe we had met the only lawyer in the world whose personality wasn't a natural contraceptive.

For a nanosecond Maddy thought about his reasons before she nodded. Who cared why he wanted to take the case? The man was willing to represent her at a more than sixty-six percent discount. But sixty-six percent of what? She forced herself to press. "I need a dollar amount, Tony. Of course, I realize it can change—will change—but without a hard number I can't wrap my head around it." Mentally, she crossed her fingers.

"For you, my retainer is ten thousand up front, and the sooner I get it the faster I can get the experts out there gathering evidence. Is that going to be a problem?"

Hell yes, that's gonna be a problem, she thought, but she wasn't about to tell him that and ruin her best chance to beat the murder rap. "I can get a check to you in a few days," she responded, already thinking of places to begin looking for the money.

Her mother used to say you couldn't get blood out of a turnip, and it was never so true as it was now. She only had two grand left in her savings account after paying for the remodel. She'd have to see about borrowing against her 401K, something she'd sworn never to do. That money was earmarked for Jess's college fund.

Pirelli took a sip of his coffee. "You do know you won't be able to use any of the twenty-five grand that showed up in your bank account last week, right?"

She sighed. "I had completely forgotten about that. I have no idea how it got there," she said, praying he believed her. Although he'd basically said it didn't matter if she was guilty or not, for some reason it was important that this man be convinced of her innocence.

"I'm working on that," he said before pulling out a file from his briefcase and spreading the papers on the table in front of him. While he looked them over, Maddy used the time to do the same to him.

About six-two with a body that screamed gym membership, Anthony Pirelli had dark wavy hair cut just above his ears and smoky brown eyes that seemed to look right through you. Dressed in a charcoal suit with a light gray shirt and matching tie, he could've stepped right out of any TV legal drama. Maddy had yet to see him really smile, but somehow, she knew it would make her weak at the knees.

"Can you think of anybody who would want to hurt you, Maddy?"

She forced her eyes back up to his face, embarrassed to have been caught looking. "Tessa thinks it's more about me being an easy mark rather than someone having a personal grudge against me." Too late she realized her mistake and clamped her lips shut.

"Tessa?"

"I'm sorry. Tessa is my sister who died last year. I don't know why I said her name. I meant to say my sister Lainey. She's married to Sheriff Winslow."

You're forgetting that I was married to Colt, too, Tessa reminded her. *Apparently, the good sheriff has a thing for the Garcia girls.*

"Hmm. We might be able to use that to our advantage when we ask for information from that department." He picked up a picture of Bernardi lying dead on the cellblock floor. "And you didn't know this man before the other night?"

"Actually, I did, but only because we've booked him several times before on a variety of charges, most of them stemming from drinking way too much booze and throwing a fist. Usually, he was out before the ink dried on his paperwork."

"And why was this time different?"

She shrugged. "Bernardi said his lawyer was somewhere in the Caribbean."

"You talked to Bernardi?"

She wondered if she should tell him about how the man had hit on her, then decided against it. "Briefly when I took him a late night snack." When the lawyer looked confused, she added, "He was diabetic."

"What'd you talk about?"

His boner! The man was arrogant enough to think he might get laid.

No way Maddy was telling him that. "He mentioned that the guy in the next cell had hit on his girlfriend. Apparently, that's what started the brawl at the bar." She lifted her cup and drained what was left of the coffee before adding, "That's the first time I'd ever really spoken to him."

"You're sure about that?" He studied her intently.

"Positive. Outside of a jail cell, I'd never seen nor spoken to the man before."

Pirelli shuffled through the papers and pulled out several sheets, staring at them momentarily before displaying them in front of her. "Then how do you account for this?"

She stared. A rush of apprehension so gripping it made her lightheaded raced through her body. Colt had been right. Bernardi's death was not the action of a small time killer looking to conveniently put the blame on her. There was a way more sinister reason why the man had been killed, and she had the sinking feeling she'd been part of a well-planned execution all along.

Picking up the paper in front of her, she studied the dead man's phone records, horrified to see her number highlighted on four separate occasions. "I swear I've never spoken to Bernardi on the phone for any reason," she said, her voice barely a whisper now.

Pirelli slid a picture across the table. "So you can explain this?"

An audible gasp escaped her lips before she could stop it. There in front of her, in black and white, was the unmistakable image of Gino Bernardi standing outside her front door talking to her daughter.

Chapter Eight

Maddy stared at the photo, unable to speak. What was her Jessie doing on their porch talking to Bernardi? And when had this happened?

Oh God! She had to talk to her daughter right now—had to make sure Bernardi hadn't said or done anything inappropriate. Surely, Jess would have told her if he had.

"So you're saying you had no idea the dead man visited your house?"

Maddy turned sharply to face Tony Pirelli. She'd been so worried about seeing Bernardi chatting it up with Jess, she'd almost forgotten her lawyer was sitting across the kitchen table and interviewing her about killing a man.

"I need to talk to my daughter," she said, reaching for her cell phone before remembering that Jessie was in school. As much as she wanted answers, calling her out of class after what happened a few nights before would only scare her more. It would have to wait until she got home.

Maddy shoved the phone back into her purse before pushing away from the table and walking over to the sink. She poured herself another cup of coffee then remembered her manners. "Want a refill?"

Tony shook his head. "No thanks. I have to be in court in Dallas at two." He glanced at his watch. "We don't have much time left." Moving the picture of Jessie and Bernardi to the side, he pointed to the dead man's phone records. "And you have no recollection of ever speaking with this man before the other night at—"

"Never," she interrupted. "I would know if..." Her eyes widened as she suddenly remembered something that might be relevant. "I'd almost forgotten about the wrong numbers. I never thought anything of it until just now, but I have been getting a few lately." She rubbed the area above her right eye as if that would magically produce a reason why her number was on the sheet in front of her. "A man asked to speak to a Francis something or other."

"All four times?" He pointed to the records again.

She blew out a breath, hating that she couldn't remember all the details of something that was so important now. "I think so."

"Can you remember when you got these wrong numbers? Specifically, I'm wondering if any of them correlate with the calls made to your cell from Bernardi's phone?"

She shrugged. "I can't be sure, although I do recall getting one after midnight on a weekday. I was ready to give someone a piece of my mind for waking me up, and it was a wrong number."

Tony studied the phone records before a half smile spread across his face. "One of the calls was made last week at two fifteen in the morning."

"That must be it," she said, excited and feeling a bit vindicated until she noticed that the smile on her lawyer's face had faded. "What?"

"Unfortunately, there's no way to prove this was a wrong number." He studied the sheet again. "Can you think back to then. Why did you stay on the line for three minutes?"

She grabbed the phone records out of his hand. "I vaguely remember now that he insisted this Francis person was there and that he really needed to talk to him. He was argumentative and persistent, and when I couldn't get him to believe that whoever he was looking for wasn't here, I hung up on him."

"That's not a lot to go on, but at least it'll give me something to work with." He gathered up the papers and put them into his briefcase. "I'll come back at the end of the week to report on any progress we make." After picking up the briefcase, he walked to the door before turning once again to face Maddy. "I'll need that check by then."

She nodded. For a few minutes after he was gone, she stared at the door. How in the hell was she going to come up with that kind of money by the end of the week?

* * * * *

Jake Matthews pulled up to the Cowboys Galore Bar and Grill, noticing the parking lot was already crowded, despite the fact it was only a little after one in the afternoon. Even for him that was a tad too early to start boozing it up.

He parked his pickup between two others, glad his three-year old F150 didn't stand out like a sore thumb. In his line of work staying low key was vital. He locked the door with a click and headed for the bar. No sooner had he walked in when he noticed two men involved in a loud debate by the pool table. Seems one of them thought the other was cheating. Before they came to blows, they must've worked it out because in no time they were back at the game like nothing had happened.

Jake took a special interest in one of them, recognizing him from the few occasions he'd been at the bar spying on Gino Bernardi. He decided to find out if the guy knew Gino.

After sauntering over to where they were, he slid onto a barstool directly in front of the billiards table. Motioning to the bartender, he ordered a beer then took a long sip before swiveling around, pretending to be interested in the game.

The shorter of the two men, the one he didn't recognize, had on a pair of jeans and a tank top. The one he had noticed a few times before in the bar was dressed in typical Texas cowboy gear; tight black jeans and a button-down plaid shirt. Jake grinned as he realized he was wearing a nearly identical outfit. He'd bet money this guy drove one of the pickups parked beside his own in the parking lot.

He decided to make his move. "Nice break," he said after the man started a new game, sending four balls into the pockets.

The cowboy tipped his hat. "Lucky shot." He turned back in time to see his opponent miss one before addressing Jake once again. "You play?"

Jake laughed. "Let's say I play at it. If I only had half your skills, I'd be happy." Okay, that was laying it on a little thick, but he had a job to do, and nobody could resist a little buttering up.

This cowboy was no different. He grinned before calling the eight ball in the side pocket and then sending it there after a double bank that could only be described as awesome.

Jake whistled, thoroughly impressed. "Yes, sir, you do have game. How about I buy you a drink for letting me watch and learn?"

"No redneck worth his salt would ever turn down a free drink." The cowboy waved his arm for the bartender. "Randy, I'll have a Scotch rocks and put it on this guy's tab." He extended his hand. "Carter Jackson. And you are?"

Jake shook his hand. "Jake Matthews. I'm new in town and thought what better place to get the skinny than at the local bar. You come here often?"

"Often enough. What kind of information you looking for?" A minute after the bartender brought the drinks over, Carter tapped his empty glass on the wooden bar to get his attention again. "Randy, bring me a double Scotch and another beer for my friend here."

"For starters, I need a place to stay. Do you know of a decent hotel that doesn't cost an arm and a leg around here?"

The cowboy squinted in deep thought. "There's a place right off Highway 114 that you might try. I've heard it's reasonable." He grinned. "Also heard it was nicknamed No-Tell Motel, if you get my drift."

Jack laughed. "Oh yeah! I've been to a few of those myself over the years."

Carter tsked. "Haven't we all?"

"So I take it this bar is a good place to hang out?"

"One of the best." Carter said before throwing back his head and draining his glass.

"Heard there was a brawl in here the other night. Were you here?"

"Not sure I'd call it a brawl. Some short dude made the mistake of pinching a girl's ass right in front of her way bigger boyfriend. Things got ugly in a hurry for the little guy before the cops came and broke it up."

Jake motioned to the bartender for another round. This conversation was beginning to get interesting, and more liquor couldn't hurt.

After the bartender set the full drink in front of his new friend, Jake decided to quit beating around the bush and get right to his questions. "Did you know any of the guys involved in that fight?"

Carter took a sip, licked his lips, then reached for a pretzel from the bowl in front of him. "The big guy's a regular here, but I'd never seen the other dude before." He shoved the pretzel into his mouth before turning to Jake. "Heard they were both shot in their jail cells that night?"

Now we're talking, Jake thought. And it had only taken three drinks.

"Seriously? How'd that happen?" he asked innocently.

"Apparently the cop on duty..." His eyes widened as he stopped talking and stared across the room, his mouth gaping open.

Jack did a one-eighty to see what had caught Carter's attention. A man and a woman were standing at the other end of the bar talking to the bartender.

He let out a soft whistle before he could stop himself, allowing his eyes to take an inventory of the woman's body. The first word that popped into his brain was hot. About five-eight with dark hair that fell to her shoulders, she filled out the turquoise sweater nicely and the black jeans that hugged her slim hips showed off even more curves. Though he couldn't see her eyes, he imagined they were as dark as her hair. He'd always been a sucker for dark eyes.

Tearing his gaze from her, he turned back to Carter when he realized the man with her had on a uniform. He'd come this far without screwing up and he had no desire to do so now. The last thing he needed was to be noticed, particularly by a police officer trained to pick up on minor details that the average Joe didn't.

"What were you saying about the man who was in the bar fight the other night?"

Carter had just chugged three shots of Scotch and would be slurring his words soon. Jake had to find out the rest of the story.

"That's the cop."

"What cop?"

Carter leaned closer and whispered, "The one who killed the guy in the jail cell the other night."

Jake's curiosity got the best of him and he twisted around for another look. "Are you saying that the guy at the other end of the bar is the one who killed the man from the fight the other night?"

"Not the guy, the chick. She's a cop, too. It was all over the news this weekend."

Jake knew his mouth most have dropped wide enough for an NFL quarterback to practice precision passing. He'd spent all day Friday trying unsuccessfully to get the facts about his mark getting killed in jail. Nobody was talking and he couldn't just walk into the police station and ask questions without drawing attention to himself. So he'd gone back to the hotel and pretty much partied all weekend with some blonde, not bothering to watch any TV or read the newspapers.

Lately, that scenario was happening more and more, and frankly, ending up in his room the next day with a woman whose naked body was the only thing he knew about her, along with one helluva hangover was starting to take its toll. Despite his penchant to stay shit-faced, he'd always prided himself on keeping his investigative skills honed. It looked like even that was heading south.

He was about to question Carter further when the lady cop looked up and met his gaze.

Damn! Her eyes were as dark as a Texas prairie on a moonless night. He couldn't stop himself and smiled.

So much for staying under the radar.

Chapter Nine

Maddy surveyed the inside of Cowboys Galore the minute she and Tom Rogers walked into the bar. Although she didn't anticipate trouble, she was unarmed and more than a little nervous. When she became a person of interest in Gino Bernardi's death, she'd been forced to give up both her badge and her service weapon. She felt naked without them and hoped the little bit of Tae Kwon Do she'd learned from her ten-year-old daughter wouldn't be necessary.

Located on the south side of town, Cowboys Galore had been serving drinks in Vineyard for as long as Maddy could remember. It catered to a loyal group of locals, most of whom had been patronizing the bar for years. On Friday and Saturday nights some aspiring country band would show up and play a few sets. The bar reminded her of the one in the TV sitcom *Cheers* where everybody knew your name. That might prove helpful when she and Rogers interviewed the customers in their search for answers.

The bar itself curled around the entire length of the room and featured a flat screen TV directly in the center above the rows and rows of liquor bottles. On either end there was a cage with a pole in the center. It didn't take a genius to know what these were for, even though there were no cowgirls dancing in skimpy outfits at the current time.

Actually, the only female besides her was a brunette sitting by herself one stool over nursing a beer. The way she was dressed suggested she might be looking to hook up and probably make some money while she was at it.

Maddy quickly scolded herself for being so judgmental. She'd always been proud of the fact that she gave everyone the benefit of the doubt. Now wasn't the time to get high and mighty. After all, her own sister had probably bedded every man in Vineyard at one time or another.

Where was Tessa anyway? She always seemed to disappear when Maddy needed her the most. If anyone knew how to sweet talk the bartender, it definitely was her.

Sitting around the bar were several men enjoying a brew either alone or with a fellow afternoon drinking buddy watching last night's hockey game rebroadcast on ESPN. Maddy felt reasonably safe in going with her gut and thinking that none of them posed a problem. At the other end, two men were playing pool and stopped to glance up when she and Rogers walked in. The way the taller of the two sneered at her had her reaching for her gun before remembering that it was locked up at the police station. She decided it might be a good idea to keep her eye on that one, just in case.

Then her gaze settled on a guy sitting on the far end of the bar. At first she thought he was also a participant in the billiards game, but then decided he was merely an observer. A longer look told her that he probably towered over six feet and was definitely easy on the eyes. Wearing a dark long-sleeved shirt and jeans that hung nicely over his boots, the guy was watching her intently, causing a warm feeling to skitter up her neck.

With sandy blond hair that curled at his ears and eyes that seemed to undress her even from that distance, he could only be described as a hottie. The Big and Rich song that Gino Bernardi had quoted when he'd tried to snag a quickie with her the night he was killed popped into her head. "Save a Horse (Ride a Cowboy)" he'd said. It made way more sense now as she tried but couldn't tear her eyes away from the eye candy at the end of the bar. Involuntarily, the flush moved from her neck to her cheeks, making her feel like a shy teenager.

And then the man smiled at her!

Quickly, she jerked her body back around to face Rogers, who was now standing against the bar conversing with the bartender. She chastised herself for acting like a "girl" and took two steps forward to stand beside Rogers, purposely keeping her back to the other end of the bar where she could feel the intense stare of the guy with the eyes that she would bet were still undressing her.

She slid between Rogers and the sexy brunette, who looked amazing in a bright yellow halter top. She'd just finished off an O'Doul's and was waving her hand to get the bartender's attention.

Non alcoholic beer is worthless, Tessa said, suddenly appearing and moving to the other side of the woman. ***It's***

like a vibrator without batteries. It will definitely fill you up, but you don't get the buzz.

Maddy bit her lower lip to keep from smiling, wondering where her sister came up with some of the things she said.

"So you were working the other night when the police were called in because of a rumble?" Rogers asked.

"I wouldn't call it a rumble. Some short guy got a little too friendly with a big guy's girlfriend, that's all. The dude didn't stand a chance. Lucky for him a few of the regulars pulled the other guy off before he ended up in the emergency room—or worse."

"Were either of the two guys regulars?" Maddy asked. When he turned to her with a question in his eyes she explained, "I'm working undercover on this one."

He gave her an appreciative nod after his eyes moved up and down her body, making her wish she hadn't worn the blue sweater that had shrunk a tad when Jessie had mistakenly thrown it into the dryer last week. "I've seen the big guy and his girlfriend in here before, but that was the first time the shorter one's graced us with his presence, at least to my knowledge."

"In your opinion, was it simply a bar fight between two strangers that got out of hand, or did you think the two men knew each other?" She edged closer wondering if the cute guy was still staring but afraid to turn around and find out.

The bartender swiped a wet rag over the surface of the bar before setting a brand-new bottle of O'Doul's in front of the brunette. "I don't think they knew each other because the bigger guy didn't call him by name. Actually called him dickhead, if I'm remembering correctly, for making a pass at the woman, which was kind of unusual in itself."

"Unusual, how?" Maddy asked, her interest piqued.

"I don't know. Maybe it's just a gut feeling, but I'd had my eye on the big guy for a few weeks. I couldn't seem to figure him out. Usually, he came in by himself and sat at one end of the bar. Before long the woman, whose honor he was defending that night, would wander in and find a seat at the other end." He stopped to point in that direction, and Maddy resisted the urge to look that way.

"She always wore clothes that captured the attention of every redneck in here, and trust me when I say she was never by herself for long. At least two or three cowboys would hot-foot it her way to be the first to buy her a drink."

"That's weird," Maddy said, squinting her eyes. "Do you think the big guy and the lady just hooked up that night and he got a little hacked that the stranger was interrupting his turn with her?"

The bartender shrugged. "Hard to tell. All I know is that I've seen the lady walk out of the bar with at least four different guys on four separate occasions, and it never seemed to bother the man before that night. And you can bet that if I noticed the little indiscretions playing out, he did, too. The dude had to know she wasn't the kind of girl you take home to your mother."

Oh please! Look around, Bozo. Most of these losers in here aren't worth the effort, even for a girl like that, unless there was an exchange of the green paper with presidents on them. They're all lucky the old saying 'Beauty is in the eyes of the beer holder' is true. Otherwise, none of these yahoos would ever have a long-term sexual relationship with anyone except Rosie Palm and her five sisters. Tessa paused before pointing to the other end of the bar. *Except for maybe that tall one down there who can't seem to take his eyes off my sister, the cop.*

Maddy turned that way, only to find the good-looking guy still staring at her. This time, though, his unsmiling eyes seemed to be boring a hole into her, as if he were trying to figure her out. Quickly she glanced back toward the bartender.

"Then why did you think the woman was his girlfriend?" Roger asked, trying not to make it obvious that he was staring at the brunette's cleavage, which was pretty impressive. Maddy couldn't help but wonder where she bought her push-up bras.

"Because he told the other guy if he ever touched his woman again, he'd kill him."

"Hmm. That's strange. He actually called her his woman?"

When the bartender nodded, Rogers turned to Maddy. "Any more questions?"

She thought about it for a minute. "Do you happen to know this woman's name?"

"I think he called her Kristi or Sissy. Something like that. I can tell you, though, that she has big blond hair and enough jewelry to start her own pawn shop. Sorry I can't be more help. Now if you'll excuse me, I see several thirsty guys who are about to start a mutiny." He grabbed two Bud Lights from under the bar and headed in the direction of the two cowboys sitting several stools over. They were definitely looking unhappy and now getting vocal with their demands.

Maddy, ask this slut puppy about the woman, Tessa said. *I saw her whole body stiffen when the bartender talked about the other chick.*

Maddy swiveled to face the brunette who was working hard at pretending not to be interested. "Did you know the woman we're talking about from the other night?"

The brunette shook her head and quickly chugged the rest of her O'Doul's.

That's bullshit, Tessa said. *I saw the way she reacted when you asked what the other lady's name was. She knows who you're talking about, Maddy. I'm sure.*

Maddy inched closer and stood there until the woman finally glanced up. "I'd hate to have to take you down to the police station for this information, but I will if I have to. All I'm asking for is a name."

The woman hesitated for only a minute. "I don't know anything about—"

Maddy grabbed her arm and lifted her off the bar stool. "Let's see if a trip downtown will jog your memory."

She hoped Tessa was right. Otherwise, she was harassing this women for no good reason, other than the fact that she liked to sit at a bar in the middle of the afternoon drinking fake beer—and quite possibly, hooking. But Maddy wasn't vice and couldn't care less how the woman paid her rent.

"Wait," the brunette said squirming out of Maddy's hold. "I'm not sure, but I think the woman you're talking about may live down the street from me. If she's the one I'm thinking about, her name is Chrissy Rockford."

Told you she knew who you were talking about, Tessa said, obviously proud of herself. *Now ask her where she buys her bras. Gravity's a bitch, big sister.*

* * * * *

"So what'd you think?" Rogers asked, as soon as they left the bar.

"I don't know. It's probably nothing." Maddy blew out a breath. "You know how guys can get when they've had a little too much to drink and someone looks at them funny. All of a sudden they think they're Rocky Balboa."

"Yeah, but the bartender said he called her his woman right before he decked the guy."

"My guess is that a lot of guys at the bar probably called her that at one time or another. Seems like she got around," Maddy said, already thinking about how she and her sisters would approach Chrissy Rockford.

"Yeah, that's true. I'll let Colt know this was probably a dead-end so we can concentrate on another angle."

They reached her car first, and she turned to face him. "Like what?"

"Like why the dead guy wore a Rolex watch and carried five grand into a bar, for starters. There's got to be something up with that."

"I'm sure if there is, you'll find it." She leaned over and gave him a peck on the cheek. "Thanks for letting me tag along, Tom."

He grinned down at her. "It's not like I volunteered to bring you, you know."

She laughed. "Small price to pay for my silence about your hot diner girl." She opened the car door and slid in.

Already planning her next move with a visit to Chrissy Rockford, she passed by Roger's car and waved. Although she and her sisters would definitely check out the woman, she cautioned herself not to get too hopeful. There was only a slim chance that the lady of the night might be able to give them anything that could help her defense.

More than likely she was simply a barfly, or "Queen of the Silver Dollar," as the Dr. Hook song proclaimed, and she probably used Cowboys Galore as an alternative to walking the streets. All those good old boys would be like a smorgasbord to her, especially after they got liquored up and listened to their small heads when there was the possibility of getting a quick blow job before going home to a wife and six kids.

As if a light bulb went off in her head, she thought back to a conversation she'd had with Bernardi before he died. He'd mentioned that Maddy would have to be a superstar in the sack since his Chrissy was one helluva contortionist. It was too much of a coincidence to ignore. Maddy smiled as she turned the corner on Main Street, thinking she finally had a solid clue to pursue.

Her mind still on how she would approach the woman, she nearly missed the hardware store and swerved at the last minute into the parking lot. She'd made a decision after her lawyer had left earlier that day. She'd do whatever was necessary to get the money for his retainer. It was now or never.

As much as she hated the idea, the entire upper floor of her house was sitting empty, waiting for her to get the extra cash to decorate the front bedroom for Jessie. There were actually two bedrooms upstairs and a full bath, and if she could get a couple of college kids or maybe even a flight attendant or two to rent from her, that would definitely make her life easier.

Jessie would be disappointed. She'd been waiting ever since the remodeling was finished to move from the tiny bedroom downstairs to her own private digs upstairs. But she'd understand. Besides, it was only temporary, and as soon as Maddy was cleared of Bernardi's murder, things would go back to their normal live–from–paycheck–to–paycheck routine.

She parked the car and nearly sprinted to the store, thinking if she didn't just go and do it, she'd change her mind. Thirty minutes later, she emerged with the biggest ROOM FOR RENT sign they had and was already thinking what else she could do to stimulate her cash flow.

Too bad she couldn't use the twenty-five grand that whoever was trying to frame her had deposited into her bank account.

Then there was the little issue of finding out from her daughter why Tony Pirelli had an eight-by-ten of her talking to Bernardi on their porch. If anyone was counting, that made twice now that her daughter had been in close proximity to a really bad guy.

What the hell kind of cop was she that she couldn't even protect her own daughter?

Driving home, she thought about how one goes about renting out a room in one's house. What would she say to the people who she absolutely did not want around her daughter without provoking a discrimination suit?

And was there a renter's agreement she could download from the Internet? Would it be simple enough for someone of her pay grade to figure out? Maybe this was something she could ask her hot new lawyer.

Thinking about how Tony Pirelli had looked that morning in his charcoal gray suit—a suit she was sure had not come off a rack—made her smile. After going through all these months without even one date, what was going on with her libido? In the course of twenty-four hours, she'd already thought seriously about getting it on with not one, but two complete strangers.

Maybe she was more like the brunette at the bar than she wanted to believe.

Or—oh, dear Lord—my sister.

Chapter Ten

Rolando Soliz smiled at Mary Ellen Davidson when he passed the nurses' station with a cart full of clean linen. For the entire two weeks he'd been on the job at Vineyard Regional Hospital he'd had his eye on the petite young nurse. With her strawberry blond hair and all those freckles sprinkled across the bridge of her nose, she was the proverbial girl next-door—and definitely virginal. He'd overheard her telling one of the other nurses how she believed in one man, one marriage.

Too bad he wouldn't see her again after today. He'd have loved to have had a taste of that sweet body.

Turning the corner he continued down the hall and immediately saw Jeff Flanagan sitting outside Room 402. Rolando didn't anticipate any problems with the cop this morning, since he and Jeff had become friends of sorts. He'd done his homework, so chatting up the cop assigned to guard the prisoner in that room had been a piece of cake from the start. Pretending to be a single father himself, Rolando had dropped a casual remark about how hard it was to spend Thanksgiving without his son. And voila! He'd created an instant connection.

He and his boss had been planning today's details for several weeks, and so far, his part had gone off without a hitch. Rolando had been hired on the spot when he'd applied for the job at Regional a week ago. With fake credentials from several East Coast hospitals, and a nursing home administrator willing to pad his resume after he'd sweet-talked his way into her bed, he'd been a shoe-in.

Seems orderlies were at a premium these days. One look at his six-foot frame and chiseled upper arms and the director of nurses had him signing on the dotted line even before she'd checked his references. By the time she finally got around to verifying his resume, he'd be long gone.

"Hey, Sergeant Flanagan," he said, rolling the cart up next to the cop. "How's it going today?"

Jeff Flanagan looked up from the crossword puzzle he was working on and smiled when he recognized Rolando. "Hey, my man, things are good. Foxworthy's been screaming all morning for more drugs, though. The guy's worse than my five-year old when it comes to pain."

Rolando nodded. "I hear you. Get ready for more bellyaching. I'm about to clean him up before lunch." He pushed the door open with the cart and headed into the room.

Alan Foxworthy opened his eyes long enough to grunt. "Oh no you don't. I hurt too damn bad to let you anywhere near me. I'm still in misery from that walk you tortured me with earlier." He shook his head. "Get out of my room."

"How do you ever expect to get back to normal if you stay in that bed all day?" Rolando opened the door to the nightstand and pulled out a basin. After filling it with warm water, he brought it over and set it down. Leaning over the bed, he whispered, "I trust you told that cop what you were supposed to about getting shot in your jail cell, right?"

Foxworthy's eyes flew open, and he stared at the orderly. "How do you know about that?"

Rolando laughed. "You don't seriously think the man would put you in the hospital without a little backup, do you?"

Although Foxworthy shook his head, his eyes remained skeptical and never once left Rolando's face.

Rolando pulled out a cell phone and dialed a number before hitting the Speaker button and laying it on the stand that stretched across Foxworthy's bed. After a few rings, a familiar voice answered.

"I'm here with Foxworthy, boss," Rolando announced.

"Terrific. No problems with the cop?"

"None. It was almost too easy," he said, sneaking a glance over his shoulder to make sure Flanagan hadn't overheard him talking.

"Cops think they're so damn smart." There was a chuckle on the other end. "So, Alan, I wanted to congratulate you on a job well done."

Foxworthy perked up. "Yeah, boss, but I never counted on Bernardi beating the shit out of me. Thought someone would intervene way before I got hammered."

"That was a chance we took, Alan—a chance you took when you accepted the stack of bills I handed you."

Foxworthy attempted to sit up and fell back onto the pillow, squealing in pain.

The door opened in a flash and Flanagan rushed in. "Everything all right in here?"

Rolando quickly covered the phone with a towel before making eye contact with Flanagan. "Alan just tried to sit up too quickly." He pointed to the basin of warm water. "And we haven't even started his bath yet." He rolled his eyes.

Flanagan smirked, then turned and walked out of the room, closing the door behind him.

"Coast is clear, boss," Rolando said as soon as he felt sure the cop was back in his chair and working on the puzzle again.

"Sorry about the gunshot wound, Alan," the voice continued. "Rolando tells me you're coming around nicely."

"If you call shitting in a bag coming along nicely, then hell yes, I am. I thought you were only going to shoot me in the arm or leg. Your dumbass girlfriend aimed directly at my stomach. The freaking bullet tore my colon in half. You didn't pay me enough for this crap." Alan's hands were shaking as his voice grew louder. "I want more money."

There was silence on the other end of the phone as Rolando reached for the syringe under the stack of towels on the cart. He knew where this conversation was headed and how it would end up. Nobody shook down the boss and walked away happy.

"Alan, I don't think you're in any position to make demands right now. We'll talk as soon as you get out of the hospital." There was a pause on the other end of the phone. "What did the sheriff say when you told him it was the lady cop who killed Bernardi and shot you?"

"What do you think he said. He didn't want to believe me. The cop is his sister-in-law." He stopped to take a sip of water and then wiped his mouth before continuing, "Listen, man, I've done everything you've asked me to and more. You said I'd only spend one night in jail and take a bullet in the arm. You haven't lived up to your end of the deal so far. This morning the doc told me that I'm looking at one more surgery—maybe two—to reconnect my goddamn bowel after it heals. Who's gonna pay for that, huh?"

"I told you I'd take care of you. Like I said, we'll talk when you get out of the hospital. My guess is they'll release you without sending you back to jail."

"You'd better make damn sure that's what happens. Another night in that jail cell and I might be coerced into singing like a bird, if you get my drift." Alan grabbed his abdomen and grunted. "Dammit, Rolando, don't just stand there. Get me some freaking drugs."

"Boss?" Rolando was already pulling up the medicine into the syringe.

"Do it."

Before Foxworthy could comprehend what was about to go down, Rolando shoved the needle into the rubber stopper on his IV tubing and injected the sodium potassium with one swift push. Grabbing a towel he covered the man's mouth so he couldn't scream. Although Foxworthy struggled, he was no match for Rolando, and in less than a minute, his body bucked and then went limp. It didn't take a neurosurgeon to know that Alan Foxworthy would never be in pain again and sure as hell wouldn't be doing any bird imitations any time soon.

Rolando emptied the unused bathwater and stood silently in the back of the room waiting, knowing that Flanagan would get suspicious if he finished up with Foxworthy's morning care too quickly. When he figured enough time had elapsed, he shoved the cart through the door and followed behind. Flanagan was concentrating on the crossword puzzle and didn't even bother to look up.

He wheeled the cart down the hall toward the nurses' lounge, knowing the room would be empty since this was the busiest time of the day on the unit. Grabbing his jacket, he headed for the door and walked to the elevator. On the ride down, he patted the airline ticket tucked into his coat pocket to make sure it was still there. When the elevator stopped on the ground floor, he did exactly what he'd done every day for the past two weeks. He waved to the security guard chatting with one of the EMTs who had just brought in a patient. Then he smiled to himself and walked through the ER automatic doors.

Before he reached his SUV, he looked over his shoulder for one last look at the hospital before sliding into the front seat and turning the key. Steering the car into traffic, he headed for DFW airport. The boss had made all the arrangements for a first class seat on the first leg of a trip that would take him to a six-room villa. There, he would find a dark-skinned call girl waiting to welcome him to beautiful Mexico City.

* * * * *

Jake kept a little more than two car lengths between him and the lady cop. This wasn't the first time he'd tailed someone, and he knew the tricks of doing it without getting made. As a cop, the woman's observational skills would be honed more than the average person's. The last thing he needed was for her to notice him following her.

He'd waited in his car halfway down the block while she went into the hardware store, confused when she'd come out carrying some kind of big sign. Although he was too far away to see what is said, he was curious why someone who had supposedly killed a man in cold blood a few nights before would need a yard sign. Was she already anticipating going to jail and having to sell her house?

When she pulled into the garage on a street in an older neighborhood in Vineyard, he made sure he was far enough away that she wouldn't notice his pickup as he eased the vehicle to the curb. Looking around, he figured the houses on the street to be in the middle income range with some newer than others. The home the woman entered looked to be much older, but well kept. Fresh paint, double pane windows that had been recently installed, and newer board on the fence. If all the pretty updates were recent, that could add up to big bucks fast. Replacing the many windows on a two-story house like that didn't come cheap, and the last time he'd checked, cops didn't make a ton of money.

He sat in the truck watching the house for thirty minutes and was just about to call it a day and head back to the hotel when her front door opened. She emerged, carrying the sign she'd bought at the hardware store. She chose a spot in the front yard and began to pound it into the ground. Reaching into the glove compartment, he grabbed his binoculars. With her standing directly in front of the sign, he couldn't make out what it said.

Then she bent over to pick up something in the grass, and the binoculars shifted to her backside where her slacks were now straining against a perfectly shaped bottom. He couldn't help himself and whistled, cursing the fact that the woman would be hands-off to him. Remembering the way she'd nailed him with a stare at the bar, he would've loved the opportunity to explore the possibilities. Especially if her backside was any indication of how spectacular the rest of her body would be, and he was pretty sure it would be.

When she turned and walked to the mailbox, he quickly re-focused the binoculars on the sign. ROOM FOR RENT. He scratched his head. Something didn't make sense. Earlier, he'd picked up a newspaper while she was in the hardware store and read about the murder. The article had implied the motive for Bernardi's death was money since they'd found a significant chunk of change recently deposited in her bank account. But if, as he suspected her accounts were frozen, then she'd still need more money. But renting a room in her house?

She walked up the sidewalk with the mail, stopping one last time to stare at the sign in front yard. His binoculars were trained on her face, and Jake could have sworn he saw a tear roll down her cheek. Then she disappeared into the house.

He sat out in his truck for fifteen minutes, trying to decide what his next move should be. He was being paid to find out all he could about Gino Bernardi and just because the man was dead, it didn't mean his job was over. He was on a mission. Positive the lady cop knew a lot more than she was letting on, he figured he'd do well to keep her in his sights.

As he stared at the sign in the front yard, an idea popped into his head. What better way to do that than to live under the same roof and observe her in her element?

The paper had said Madelyn Castillo was a rookie cop, widowed many years ago—a single mother raising a ten-year-old daughter. The article also said that some fancy lawyer from Dallas had agreed to defend her, and Jake knew from experience that legal help like that came with a hefty cash commitment.

He knew he was taking a chance that she might recognize him from the bar, but even if she did, he'd at least get to talk to her face to face. His commanding officer had always said that his initial impressions when he first met a person of interest were always spot on. He hoped that would be true today since he might not get the opportunity to stay close to her to watch her every move if this room thing didn't work out. He grabbed the phone from his shirt pocket and called his boss.

"Hey, Jake, I was just thinking about you. Anything new on Bernardi?"

"Not on him, but I've got a chance to chummy up with the woman accused of killing him."

"Terrific," the voice on the other end said. "If anyone knows how to get close to a woman, it's you, Jake."

Although that was meant as a compliment, for some reason, it stung. "I need a favor."

"And what's that?"

"I'm going to try to rent a room in her house to check her out and see if Bernardi shared anything with her before she killed him. I'll need to list your apartment building as my former residence. Can you get your doorman to vouch for me?"

"Done. Anything else?"

"She'll probably call you to verify that I work at the insurance company."

"Again, not a problem. The faster we can get in and out, the better. We'll do what we have to. I'll be waiting to hear how this all pans out."

After hanging up the phone, Jake started the engine, and drove the half block to the lady cop's house. He parked in front and exited the car before taking a deep breath and walking up the sidewalk to the porch.

Why was he so nervous? He'd been undercover many times before and had played many different roles. Why should this one be any different?

Fidgity fingers pushed the door bell—twice. The door inched open, and he searched her eyes for any sign the landlady cop recognized him.

"May I help you?" she asked, keeping the door half closed.

He smiled, hoping it would put her at ease. When it failed miserably, he plunged ahead. "I'm new in town and saw the sign out front. I'm wondering if you rent by the month?"

Wrinkling her brow, she pushed the door closed a little more "I'm looking for a woman tenant."

"And why is that?"

She peered at him through the tiny slit that remained. "I just think a woman would fit in better with me and my daughter."

"Look, I'm not going to be in town for long, and there's no way I want to stay in a hotel all that time. Will you at least think about it?"

She studied his face. "What were you doing at Cowboys Galore today?"

Question answered. She did remember him. "I was trying to get a lead on a place to live. Figured what better way than to ask the locals if one was available."

"Is that how you found out about my house?"

He opened his mouth to confirm before he realized she was testing him. She'd only just put the sign out and nobody would have known. "No. The only place they knew about was near downtown, but the owner wants a six month lease. That doesn't work for me since I don't plan on staying in Vineyard long." He paused. "I just happened to drive by here looking at neighborhoods."

He watched as she wet her lips before she answered. "I have two rooms upstairs, and I'd really like to get a couple of flight attendants interested. I hope you understand."

He was losing her, and he had to do something drastic.

"I'll pay for both of them," he blurted, hoping he wouldn't scare her off with his enthusiasm.

"It wouldn't be cheap."

He smiled, praying she would react like every other female when he flashed that grin. All his life he'd used it on women. Once again it didn't faze her.

"It will be worth it to get out of the stuffy hotel." He paused. "And it's only for a short time. I can give you references."

Knowing that she had access to police data banks, he felt sure she would use more than his references to check him out. She and her buddies down at the police station had access to files that no one else did.

Sensing that she might be considering it, he handed her a business card. "Where are my manners? I'm Jake Matthews. I work for Harold's of London Insurance Company out of San Antonio."

He hoped that would impress her, and he fought to suppress the grin when he saw that it had. Harold's was almost as well known as their famous counterpart that catered to the rich and famous.

"Wait here," she said before closing the door. When she returned, she had a four-page application as well as an authorization page to verify employment and rental history. "Fill this out and return it at your earliest convenience. I can't promise anything, but I will consider it."

He took the stack of papers and was about to thank her when she closed the door.

So much for his powers of persuasion. On the drive back to the hotel, he considered how to get the paranoid lady cop to trust him. Since she hadn't fallen for his ready smile, he'd have to work on Plan B.

And pray he didn't need a Plan C.

Chapter Eleven

Colt Winslow stared at the computer screen on his desk. It was the security footage taken from the cameras in the cell block on the night Gino Bernardi was murdered. Thank God those had been working. He watched a dark-haired woman in a police uniform shoot the prisoner as he jumped off the cot and scrambled around his cell trying unsuccessfully to get away from her.

After the first shot took him down, the woman opened the cell door and calmly walked in, shooting him one more time at point blank range. She'd kept her face away from the cameras as if she'd known exactly where both of them were located. Then she'd stepped over the river of blood streaming from Bernardi's head and moved to the other cell. There she'd taken aim and fired one shot into Alan Foxworthy's abdomen before calmly exiting the cell block, again shielding her face from either camera.

Dammit!

Colt was hoping the tape would prove beyond a reasonable doubt that Maddy hadn't killed Bernardi. He replayed it again, concentrating on the way the woman walked, on her mannerisms. He was looking for something—

anything that would be a clear indicator that it was someone else dressed up in a cop's uniform and not his sister-in-law.

But there was nothing unusual, and from the images of the lady's back and a few blurry shots of the front, no jury would be able to say for certain that it wasn't Maddy with the gun in her hand.

Frustrated, he slammed his fist on the desk hard enough to draw the attention of Tom Rogers who had just walked into the station. He waved to the officer to indicate that everything was alright.

But everything was not alright.

One man had been killed and another badly wounded in his jail cell, and their only suspect couldn't possibly have done it. He knew that in his gut, yet he also knew that whoever was framing Maddy for the murder had spent a lot of time preparing for that night. The plan had been too intricate and executed too perfectly for it to have been spur of the moment.

But if he believed that, then how could he explain the fact that Maddy wasn't supposed to be on duty that night? How could someone have known that Jeff Flanagan would get a call from his ex and have the opportunity to keep his kids an extra two days over the holidays? Or that Maddy would be the one who had graciously volunteered to change shifts with him?

He'd have to think more on that later, but for now, he was anxious to hear what Rogers had found out at Cowboys Galore. After waving for the officer to come to his office, Colt ran the tape back one more time. Still, nothing seemed out of the ordinary until the shooter walked away from Bernardi and stood outside Alan Foxworthy's cell. Colt hit the Stop button and ran it back again, this time in slow motion. Something about it wasn't right, but he couldn't quite put his finger on it...and it was driving him crazy.

He looked up when Tom Rogers knocked on his door and walked into the office.

"Hey, Colt, whatcha looking at?"

Colt swiveled the computer screen around for his deputy to see. "I've watched this four times already. I keep hoping something will jump out at me." He turned the screen back to face him again. "Any luck at the bar?"

"Might have gotten a lead on the woman from the other night."

"The one Bernardi and Foxworthy were fighting over?"

"Yep." Roger looked pleased with himself. "The funny thing was the bartender told us the woman had been hooking up with men there on several different occasions, and it never bothered Bernardi before that night."

Colt's eyebrow hitched. "Us?"

Rogers diverted his eyes away from Colt's narrowed ones and shifted his weight to the other leg, a maneuver Colt recognized as something his deputy always did when he was nervous.

"I was asking questions, and there was this other woman at the bar who recognized Bernardi's girlfriend from the bartender's description. She's the 'us' I was talking about." He paused and finally looked Colt in the eye. "Said she thinks the woman lives down the street from her. I ran by the house she mentioned on my way back here, but nobody was home." He shifted his weight back to the other leg. "Thought I'd stop by after work and ask her a few questions if she's home."

Colt stared at him for a moment. "And what did Maddy have to say about all this?"

Roger's eyes widened, and he shook his head quickly. Way too quickly. "Maddy? How would she know about my trip to the bar? You said we weren't supposed to tell her anything at all about the case."

"I did, indeed. I just wanted to impress upon you why giving Maddy information would be such a bad idea. I know you want to keep her in the loop, Tom, but it's for her own good that she stays as far away from this investigation as possible, at least until we can clear her name."

"She has to be going crazy not knowing what's happening down here."

"Knowing Maddy, I'm sure she is, but even if she's not thinking about her own safety, we have to. There's a shooter out there who has balls big enough to walk right into our house and kill a prisoner under our noses. And if that isn't enough, to then make sure that one of ours takes the blame for it." He shook his head. "And another thing, I'd hate to have someone's testimony thrown out because she intimidated a witness."

"She'd never do that."

Colt pursed his lips, thinking that Maddy and her meddling sisters wouldn't think twice about doing just that. As sure as he was sitting here right now, he knew that somehow Maddy was poking around in the case. Maybe she hadn't actually gone to Cowboys Galore, but he'd bet good money that she'd been the first person Rogers had called after he'd left the bar and gotten back into his patrol car.

Hell, he'd probably called her on the way out the door. And now with Tessa's ghost showing up again, it was a certainty the Garcia sisters would find a way to get involved in the murder investigation. The fact that the women had been instrumental in finding Tessa's killer had them believing they were all mini Jessica Fletchers.

But he'd have to wait to go down that road with Maddy and Lainey, positive he was spot on to include his own wife in the middle of it all. She was loyal to her sisters and would do anything if one was in trouble. And Maddy was definitely in trouble right now.

"Just wanted to be clear about what's at stake here, Tom."

Colt glanced out his window where Sherry, the woman who'd taken over as his secretary when Maddy left for the police academy the year before, was on the phone. She waved her hand in the air when she saw him looking her way.

"Why don't you bring our bar girl in and question her here at the station?" Colt stood up and walked to the door. "People are sometimes intimidated by this place and tend to be a little more honest."

Before Rogers could close the door behind him, Sherry hung up the phone and came running past both of them into Colt's office.

"That was Flanagan," she said, excited. "He said you need to get over to Vineyard Regional right away."

For a moment Colt felt a little rush of hope snake up his back. Was it possible that Foxworthy had changed his story about seeing Maddy shoot him? "Did he say why?"

"Alan Foxworthy is dead."

Colt grabbed his keys from his desk drawer and started toward the front door.

"You want me to go with you, boss?"

"No, you stay here and work on getting that woman into the interrogation room," Colt said over his shoulder. Once he was in his car, he turned on the sirens and headed for Vineyard Regional.

The minute he walked through the emergency room doors at the hospital, the feeling of doom and gloom set in. The last report he'd received from the doctor about Foxworthy had been promising. They'd expected him to be discharged in a few more days, and Colt had plans for a much lengthier interrogation when that happened. He was surprised to hear the man was dead. According to Foxworthy's surgeon, although the prisoner needed another surgery down the road and was lucky to have survived, his prognosis had been good.

Guess his luck had run out.

Colt rounded the corner and waved to one of the nurses he'd known since grade school.

"Sheriff, what do you want us to do with the body?" another nurse asked, suddenly appearing beside him.

"I'll be able to answer that after I have a chance to talk to my officer."

He proceeded down the hallway to Room 402 and was surprised to see the chair outside the room empty. Pushing open the door, his first thought was that someone had tossed the room. There was a cart next to the bed with syringes and vials strewn all over the top and EKG graph paper rippling from the monitor on top down to the floor, weirdly resembling a slinky.

He didn't need a medical degree to know what it all meant. Apparently, they'd tried unsuccessfully to revive Foxworthy. He remembered all too clearly from several years back when he'd been called home from college after his dad had been hit by a hit and run driver. They'd worked for over an hour trying unsuccessfully to keep him alive, and the room had looked very similar afterwards.

He chased that memory from his head and concentrated on the cart. The Crash Cart, they called it. *How appropriate*, he thought, scanning the mess in the room again.

The door to the bathroom opened suddenly, and instinctively, he reached for his gun before realizing it was only Flanagan.

"Hey, boss, how long have you been here?" Flanagan dried his hands and threw the paper towel into the trash can. "All the coffee the nurses have been pumping into me finally kicked in, and I didn't want to leave the room unguarded."

Colt relaxed and nodded. He took a few steps and stood next to the bed, getting his first look at Alan Foxworthy. Something about a dead man always made him uneasy, which was a real drawback, considering what he did for a living.

A breathing tube was still taped to Foxworthy's nose, although it was disconnected from the machine on the wall.

Someone had at least thought to close the dead man's eyes, and if you didn't know what had gone on in this room, you might think Foxworthy had simply drifted off to sleep.

Colt touched the hand with the IV needle still in place. It was already cold. "So what do they think happened?"

Flanagan shrugged. "The doctor said it was probably a heart attack."

"Heart attack? The guy's only in his thirties."

"I know. Doc said the stress of the surgery and everything that's happened to him over the past few days must have been too much. Said this sometimes happens even without a prior history of heart problems."

Colt took a deep breath and let it out slowly. "When did he die?"

Flanagan glanced down at his wristwatch. "The orderly cleaned him up around ten-ish, and Foxworthy was alive and well then. I came in to check on him when I heard him scream, but he was only hollering for his pain medicine."

"Did he get it?"

"What?"

"The pain med. Did someone give him morphine or some other narcotic?"

Flanagan thought for a minute. "I don't remember the nurse coming in after the orderly left. About ten or fifteen minutes later, the nurse's aide came by to take his vital signs. She's the one who found him."

"Then what happened?"

"They called a code and worked on him for about a half hour before they realized they wouldn't be able to save him.

Something about his pupils being fixed and dilated. So they stopped giving CPR."

Colt glanced up at the IV bag, noticing it was no longer dripping and the machine that regulated it was turned off. "Have you had a chance to talk to the orderly yet?"

Flanagan shook his head.

"Why not?"

"Thought I'd better wait on you. I'll go get him now and bring him back here."

"Good idea. He was the last one to see this guy alive. Maybe Foxworthy said something to him before he died that might help us with the case." Colt walked around the bed, scrunching his nose at the strong urine odor coming from the catheter bag hanging on the side.

"I'll be back in a minute," Flanagan said, before pushing open the door and walking down the hall.

Colt sat down in the chair next to the bed while he waited for Flanagan to return with the orderly. He was anxious to talk to the guy so he could get back to the station. With Foxworthy gone, the last bit of hope that maybe he would change his mind about his positive ID of Maddy was also gone.

And with the security footage that showed Bernardi's killer looking a lot like his sister-in-law, his job of proving she hadn't killed anyone just got harder.

He moved his neck in circles, trying to relieve the tension building there and his eyes caught sight of the clock next to the TV on the opposite wall. It had been over twenty minutes since Flanagan went for the orderly.

What in the hell was taking so long? He needed to get back to the station to see whether Rogers had been successful in getting the woman from the bar to come to the station and to study that security footage again. Whatever had seemed out of place to him the last time he'd looked might stand out this time. Then he remembered the department had gone high-tech the year before and everything on the computer in his office automatically downloaded to his cell phone.

After pulling it out of his pocket he followed the prompts until the image of the killer popped onto the screen. Once again he watched the woman in the uniform kill Bernardi before going after Foxworthy.

Then it hit him! Seeing it now made him wonder how he could have missed it the other four times he'd viewed the footage. It was that obvious when you were looking for it.

He pushed the Replay button then brought the phone closer to his face for a better look. He had no idea what it meant, if it even meant anything, but right before the shooter took aim at Foxworthy, the camera had caught the look on his face. A man staring up at the barrel of a gun should have been panicking and trying to get out of the killer's range. Foxworthy was doing neither. He had simply looked up, and in the split second before the gun went off, he may have even smiled.

Before Colt could process what that might mean, Flanagan burst into the room, obviously excited. "You're not gonna believe this, boss."

"Where's the orderly?" Colt asked, putting away his phone and standing up.

"That's what you're not gonna believe. They've looked everywhere. He's gone."

"What do you mean gone?"

"No one's seen him since about an hour ago, and his locker is cleaned out."

All of a sudden, everything was beginning to make sense to Colt. "Call Mark Lowell and tell him to get down here with his CSI team right away. Then cordon off this area. It looks like this room may be a crime scene."

Chapter Twelve

Anthony Pirelli stared at the report in front of him, wondering how anyone could think that Madelyn Castillo had it in her to kill a person in cold blood, even someone as sleazy as Gino Bernardi. If his new client did by chance possess hidden psychopathic tendencies, he was doing a favor for a man way more powerful than he was to find out if the prisoner had confided in her before his death. If there was even the slightest possibility that Bernardi had chatted her up the night he was killed, Tony was their best bet to find out what was said.

If she hadn't killed Bernardi, setting her up for the murder had been a stroke of genius and had required intense planning on the killer's part. He'd lay odds that the Vineyard Sheriff's Department would need a lot of help to prove her innocence, even though she was one of their own. In his opinion, the local cops were way out of their league with this case, and he hoped his client wouldn't pay the price because of it.

Proving she was innocent was a challenge since the evidence against her would be difficult to explain away. Even having spent only a little time with her, he'd already decided she was someone he'd get along with under different circumstances. But he'd have to maintain a professional relationship, at least until the trial was over.

He got up and walked to the mini-bar in the boardroom lined with multiple pictures of his dad and his *powerful* friends. After Mario Pirelli had died in his jail cell many years back, young Tony had dedicated his life to making his dad proud. And this room had been turned into a shrine in his memory.

He poured two fingers of whiskey, threw back his head, and drained it. Two in the afternoon was a little early to be drinking alone, but something about this case had him on edge.

Maybe it was the fact he'd basically been ordered to take Maddy on as a client that had him unnerved. Vineyard was a forty-minute drive from downtown Dallas where his office was located, and his plate was already filled with some high profile murder cases. Ever since he'd beaten the district attorney's best prosecutor not once, but three times on cases he shouldn't have won, he'd enjoyed a reputation as a lawyer with the best chance of getting someone off—even if that someone had been found holding the smoking gun.

He'd almost had his secretary call and say that his schedule was too tight right now to take on another case. That was before a messenger had arrived at his townhouse on Friday night with the preliminary paperwork.

And on a holiday weekend, no less. When he'd argued that his caseload already had him working eighty hours a week, they hadn't been sympathetic. Even guilted him by pointing out that his dad would have been the first one to help them if he were still alive.

Mario Pirelli had always believed his son should come up the business ladder the hard way. If adding an extra twenty hours to an already busy work schedule was necessary, he wouldn't have thought twice about making his son put in the time. The fact that Tony's social life was almost nonexistent anyway wouldn't have mattered to the old man.

What little contact Tony had with the female gender added up to a whole lot of first dates over the past six months. An expensive dinner and a lot of sweet talking usually got him breakfast in bed, but he didn't have the time or the inclination right now to work on developing a long-term relationship with any of his one night stands.

In essence, he was married to the job. Maybe that was why he'd felt a strange tightness in his groin when he'd gotten his first look at the accused cop herself. But he was pretty sure an expensive meal and a come-on smile wouldn't get him an invite into her bedroom.

Maintaining a business relationship with all his clients was essential to his success, and he'd have to be very careful around her. The story she'd related about the night Gino Bernardi was killed was hard to swallow with no evidence to support it. But in the end, he was left with no choice about taking her case. Not if he wanted to take over where his father had left off.

When the call came in from back east on Friday, Tony had a feeling his weekend plans would be shot to hell. You don't say no to "an offer you can't refuse" and walk away with intact knee caps.

Growing up in a small town in New Jersey, he'd understood about the well-dressed men who'd come to their house late at night. These weren't your average citizens seeking legal advice. And they sure as hell didn't make their money running restaurants or dry cleaning establishments. When they'd show up at the Pirelli house with their bodyguards after hours, his father would drop everything to take care of them. Even before the senior Pirelli had become the target of an FBI investigation for tax evasion, Tony had concluded that his father's clients were not your usual run-of-the-mill rich guys in silk suits.

A week after Tony's dad learned that the FBI was actively investigating him, he'd begun making plans to uproot his wife and two sons and move to Dallas. He'd been so sure the grand jury wouldn't have enough evidence against him, he'd even bought a house in a wealthy suburb. Two weeks later the indictment came down and the plans were put on hold.

After his conviction, Tony's mother wanted to stay close to her husband and refused to leave New Jersey. Shortly after that, Mario was diagnosed with an aggressive form of lung cancer and died five months later.

A year later, Tony graduated from Harvard Law School, and he, his mother, and his brother followed his father's last wish and moved to the Metroplex. With the help of his father's old friends back in Jersey, Tony had been hired as an associate with one of the most prestigious firms in Dallas.

Like the other first year associates, he'd started at the bottom and quickly worked his way up.

That had been eight years ago, and over that time he had turned the law firm into one of the most successful in the city. Soon after that, he'd put out his own shingle and now had his pick of clients, most of them rich and famous—and guilty.

His brother had majored in business and moved back to the East Coast three years ago to work with his father's old "friends." That's when Tony started getting calls from New Jersey, with requests for little favors. At first it was only things like helping a widowed woman win a lawsuit against her landlord or keeping someone's teenage son out of juvie.

And although the requests had increased lately, none were as involved as this latest one. Tony hoped it wouldn't be a precedent to future favors.

Madelyn Castillo didn't fit the profile of his usual wealthy client. She'd made it perfectly clear that it would be a challenge to scrape up enough money for the retainer even though he'd quoted her a figure that was only a fifth of what he'd normally required up front.

He'd thought it best to ask for some money to keep her from becoming overly suspicious. But what Maddy didn't know was that he'd been prepared to take her on as a pro bono client if it had come down to it. All he'd been told about the case was that the request had included a specific goal.

"Find out what the scumbag told her that night in jail. See if she knows anything about the necklace," the voice had commanded.

Necklace. Somebody in New Jersey wanted him on Maddy's defense team to find out if she knew anything about a necklace.

Must be one helluva piece of jewelry.

* * * * *

Maddy placed the French toast in front of her daughter, struggling to find the right words to ask about the picture taken on their porch. She didn't want to scare her, but she had to know why she'd been talking to Bernardi.

"Don't forget, Mom. We're going on a field trip to the Dallas Aquarium today, and I won't be home until after five," Jessie said as she poured way too much syrup over her breakfast. "Mrs. Delgado said she'd drop me off afterwards."

"I know. She called and told me. You've never been to the aquarium before, so it should be a lot of fun. Do you need extra money?" Maddy was glad her back was facing Jessie since her daughter could read her better than anyone else.

The truth was, money was tight right now, and she wouldn't get paid until Friday. Most of last week's paycheck had gone toward the ten grand retainer for her defense lawyer. Anthony Pirelli was making a second trip to Vineyard on Friday to finalize the financial arrangement and to discuss any new findings on her case. He was bringing his entire legal team to spend a couple of hours going over the details of the night Bernardi was murdered, and he'd made it clear he would need the money then.

So far she'd managed to scrape up nearly eight thousand dollars, counting the money both Lainey and Deena had contributed. She'd worry about the other two grand later. Right now she was more interested in why the police had found a picture of the dead man standing on her front porch the week before he'd been killed.

"I just need a couple of bucks for a hot dog and a soda or something." Jessie studied Maddy's face before adding, "But I can take a cheese sandwich and an apple instead."

"Who are you and where's my daughter?" Maddy joked. "You'd give up a hot dog and a Coke for a cheese sandwich?" She reached into her purse and pulled out a twenty dollar bill. "Here, sweetheart. I'm sure they'll be a special souvenir you'll want to bring home, too."

She pictured her daughter eating from a bag lunch while her classmates pigged out on all the overpriced food available at the aquarium. Cotton candy and kettle corn were half the fun of going on field trips. There was no way she'd allow Jessie to give up something like that, even if it meant pulling her own budget reins even tighter. This was her mess, and she intended to find a way to make it go away.

She'd already given up her daily Caramel Macchiato at Starbucks and figured that alone saved her over twenty bucks a week. The next thing that would have to go was cable TV. They barely had time to watch it, anyway.

A second cup of coffee in hand, she grabbed the manila folder from the counter and sat down at the kitchen table opposite her daughter. When Jessie popped the last bite of French toast into her mouth and reached for the glass of orange juice, Maddy decided it was now or never.

"Hey, sweetie, I have a question for you." She opened the folder and pulled out the picture of Bernardi and Jess on the porch. After sliding it across the table, she asked, "Do you remember talking to this man?"

She held her breath waiting for the response. If Jessie told her that Bernardi had said or done anything inappropriate, she didn't know if she'd be able to handle it. She already felt guilty enough as it was that her daughter was a latchkey kid. But afterschool care was pricey, and with Maddy occasionally doing shift work down at the station, it wasn't worth it. She'd been surprised to find out she'd have to pay the weekly fee to a day care center even when she worked the night shift and didn't need for Jessie to go there after school. She'd argued that her job required her to work all hours and they should consider that, but the school wouldn't relent. Policy is policy, they'd told her.

That's when she'd made the decision to allow her ten-year-old daughter to ride the bus home from school and to stay at home alone for the two hours before she could get there after working the day shift. Even though she insisted that Jessie call her every thirty minutes after she was in the house with the door locked, the guilt still overwhelmed her. Especially at times like this when she felt like such a bad mother.

She was so caught up in her own thoughts she didn't notice her daughter picking up the photo until after she'd laid it back down. Neither said a word but it was obvious by the look on Jessie's face that she thought she was in trouble.

"Yeah, I remember the guy."

The knot in Maddy's stomach tightened. "I told you never to open the door when I'm not here."

"I didn't, Mom. Honest. I couldn't find my notebook and thought maybe I'd dropped it on the walk from the bus to the house." Her eyes pleaded with Maddy to understand. "He pulled up in a big fancy car. I hurried to get into the house, but he just kept following me and asking questions."

"What kind of questions?"

"Stupid ones. I think he was lost or something."

Maddy closed her eyes so Jess wouldn't see the tears that had formed. That was the classic MO of a pedophile.

"He showed me a picture of some guy at a bar with a woman. Said the guy lived here."

"Oh my God, Jess, you should have run into the house and locked the door. You know I told you to call 911 if you ever felt like you were in trouble. He could've been a pervert."

"I had my phone with me, Mom. And Mrs. Rutledge was out in her yard pulling weeds. If the man had tried to grab me, I would have screamed, and she would have come immediately." Jessie leaned over and wiped the lone tear that had escaped down Maddy's face.

Maddy took a deep breath and tried to smile. No sense making this a bigger deal than it was.

"I didn't tell you because I knew you would freak—

just like you're doing right now," Jessie continued. "Besides, I only talked to him long enough to tell him there were no guys living here. I told him it was just you and me and that you were a cop. Figured that would scare him off. I even offered to call you at the station to see if you knew this Alan person he was asking about, but he got really nervous and left right after that."

Maddy's head jerked up. "Alan?"

"Yeah, that's the guy he was looking for."

Maddy scooted her chair closer to her daughter's. She had no idea why this seemed important but her police instincts kicked in and she pressed on. "Think, Jess. Did he mention the guy's last name?"

"Yes, but I've forgotten it. I remember thinking it sounded like some kind of animal." She shot up from her chair and leaned over to kiss Maddy's forehead. "Gotta run or I'll be late. Don't worry about me, Mom. I'm ten, remember?" She grabbed her backpack from the counter and headed for the door.

Maddy got up and walked out to wait with her for the school bus. Her gut told her it was too much of a coincidence that Bernardi has shown up at her house the week before she was accused of killing him. And why had the police found the photo at *his* house when they'd tossed it after his murder? He couldn't have taken it himself, so there had to have been an accomplice. But why take it at all?

And why did he think someone named Alan lived there? She'd bought the house from Barney Krieger, a widower whose children were grown and long gone. The elder Krieger had decided that the house was too much to take care of alone and he'd gone off to one of those swanky seniors-only places in North Dallas.

And if Maddy remembered correctly, he'd only had two daughters.

After hugging Jessie one last time, she watched her walk onto the bus, hiding her fears as she waved before the bus pulled away. She was beginning to get a bad feeling about all this and wished she could talk to Rogers right now. Maybe he could shed some light on all of it.

What she'd really like to do was pick up the phone and run this by her brother-in-law, but that was out of the question. She wasn't in the mood for one of Colt's hour-long lectures about how she'd promised to stay out of the investigation.

But how could she? This whole thing was becoming more and more personal. Someone had deliberately set her up and had worked really hard at it the week before Bernardi was killed. They'd made contact with her ten-year old, for God's sake!

Even though she'd only talked to Gino Bernardi briefly, she had no doubt the man couldn't have known he'd be shot that night. He'd been so confident he'd be getting sprung from jail by morning, he'd even invited her to a steak dinner—served with an orgasm for dessert—the next night. Plus he was way too egotistical to agree to a plan that ended up with him dead.

No, either someone had double crossed him and decided to conveniently tie up a loose end, or he was merely an innocent pawn in an intricate plan to blackmail her. But if he was a loose end, that meant the other guy in the cell next to him could have been the target all along.

Dammit! She racked her brain trying to remember the other prisoner's name, but she kept coming up blank.

She turned and walked back to the house. With only half an hour before her sisters would arrive to decide what their next move would be, she needed to grab a quick shower. Halfway up the steps, she froze in her tracks.

Then she sprinted back to the kitchen and grabbed the manila folder. Flipping through the pages, she finally found what she was looking for. There in black and white on the police report was the name of the guy who had positively ID'ed her as the person who had shot him at the police station.

Alan Foxworthy.

She shook her head as if she could get rid of the confusing thoughts overwhelming her right now. She'd never believed in coincidences, and she wasn't about to start now.

The fact that Gino Bernardi had been looking for someone with the exact name of the guy he'd fought with at Cowboys Galore and had ended up next to him in a Vineyard jail cell had to mean something.

But what?

A wave of nausea pulsed through her as her daughter's words just a few minutes before came back to her. When she'd asked Jessie if she remembered the last name of the man Bernardi was looking for at their house, she'd said it sounded like an animal to her.

Everyone had assumed that Bernardi hadn't known the guy he'd nearly killed in the bar that night. What if both of them had been part of the setup?

Chapter Thirteen

Deena bit down on a breakfast burrito and reached for a second one from the opened box in the center of the table. "Rosa's Cantina makes the absolute best breakfast burritos in town. It was a great idea to order in, Maddy."

"Lainey brought these." Maddy placed a nearly full bottle of orange juice and four glasses on the table. "Help yourselves."

"Then kudos to Lainey," Deena said. "Thanks, sis. I needed this."

"You're welcome." Lainey reached for a burrito before they were all gone. "I figured Maddy had her hands full trying to prove she didn't kill Bernardi. Besides, Rosa's was right on the way, and I had a couple of two-for-one coupons from the other night when Colt, Gracie, and I ate there."

"After all the hospital food I've eaten for the past couple of days, this tastes like I've died and gone to Mexican food heaven." Kate poured on the hot sauce before shoving the last bite of burrito into her mouth.

Watching her sisters sitting around the dining room table doing what they did best—eating—Maddy felt a sudden surge of confidence. When the Garcia girls put their heads together to work on a project, nothing stopped them. Seeing them all together again gave her a renewed hope that they'd be able to get her out of the mess she was in. She remembered their success the previous year when they'd worked relentlessly to find Tessa's killer.

Maddy stopped midway through a huge bite and glanced around the room. Where was Tessa anyway? Her younger sister had always been the social butterfly of the group, and if anyone knew what went on behind closed doors in Vineyard, it was Tessa. She needed to be here with them now. Although she wished she could summon her up somehow, Maddy knew that Tessa's ghost popped in and out randomly. Even Tessa herself had no control over when she made an appearance. At least that's what she said every time they fussed about it.

Maddy glanced at the clock above the sink. It was almost ten, and she still hadn't given her sisters an update about what she'd uncovered the past two days. She couldn't wait any longer for Tessa, figuring she could bring her up to speed later. Right now, she needed to get the meeting started.

Taking a big gulp of her orange juice to wash down the last of her breakfast, she faced her sisters. "Okay, first off, we need someone to take notes." She shoved a pad and pencil Deena's way. "You've always been pretty good at that, Deena. Do you mind?"

Deena beamed like someone had just told her she looked like a million bucks—which was far from the truth, if Maddy was being honest. Her eyes were puffy making Maddy wonder if her sister was battling insomnia or eating too much salt. And her hair was about a month past due for a cut and style. Sporting a pair of slacks and a dingy white blouse that looked as though it'd been washed with a load of darks, the always spruced-up Deena hadn't even bothered to put on makeup. This was so not Deena, and it worried Maddy.

She decided she'd have a private talk with her after the others left. Although Deena was two years younger than her, they'd grown up best friends, sharing everything with each other. Both could tell how the other was feeling with just a look.

And after taking another peek, Maddy was sure something was definitely up with her sister. She wondered if whatever was bothering Deena was something recent. Or had they all been too busy with their own lives lately to notice that something had been going on with her for awhile? Regardless, she vowed to take care of that today, mentally scolding herself for not being there for her sister.

"Here's what we know so far." She proceeded to tell them about her trip to the bar with Tom Rogers, purposely leaving out the part about the hot cowboy who'd unnerved her with his intense stare.

"Something smells fishy," Kate interrupted when Maddy repeated what the bartender has said about Bernardi. "Why would the guy suddenly get bent out of shape over someone flirting with the woman when she'd obviously been using the bar to pick up guys all along?"

Maybe because he got a taste of her himself and decided to go all macho and possessive on her.

Maddy turned just as Tessa walked from the living room into the kitchen and pulled up a chair next to Deena.

Or maybe he was her pimp and didn't like the guy's attitude. Have you given any thought to that, sis? She plopped down and pointed to Deena's hair. *What's up, girlfriend? You need a new 'do.*

"I did think of that, but if it's true, why would Bernardi nearly kill the guy if he was actually her pimp? Isn't that like throwing money away?"

"What are you talking about?" the three sisters asked in unison.

"Oh, sorry," Maddy said. "I forgot I'm the only one who can hear Tessa. She's wondering if Bernardi was a pimp."

"You know, that's a real possibility," Kate said, narrowing her eyes. "But I still don't get why he was so outraged and pounded on the other guy for getting chummy if he and the girl were turning tricks together."

"From what all the witnesses at the bar said, it appeared the two men didn't know each other." Maddy shook her head. "It just doesn't add up."

"It sure doesn't," Deena said. "Why would the guy make a pass at this woman if he was about to get everything and more after he handed over some cash? No foreplay necessary when there's money involved. And didn't you tell us that Bernardi was about fifty pounds heavier, Maddy?" She waited until Maddy nodded before continuing. "So, why would the other guy grope her right in front of Bernardi if he knew there was no way he would get laid and a very real possibility he would get whaled on?"

For the same reason dogs chase cars that they have no chance in hell of catching. They're stupid. Maybe the guy had already forked out the cash and was just getting a head start on his investment. A naked woman in bed has a tendency to overpower a man's good sense. Come to think of it, that's assuming men have any sense at all, good or bad.

Maddy pondered that for a moment. "Okay, let's assume Bernardi hooked up with our mystery lady recently and was just having a testosterone reaction when he saw some guy grab her tush. That would explain why he ended up pounding the living crap out of the other guy, but it wouldn't tell us why his killing went down the way it did that night." She stared down at the picture of Bernardi. "Why would someone go to all the trouble of carrying out this execution at the station in a way that would frame me? If they'd have waited one more day, they could've killed him in the parking lot of a bar somewhere. Or at his apartment. Seems to me that would've been a whole lot easier. So why am I in the mix?"

"Yeah, we're definitely missing something," Kate said before glancing at her watch. "I have to be back at the hospital in an hour, Maddy. Is there anything else we need to talk about before I leave?"

Maddy sighed, knowing her sisters would all flip out when they found out that Bernardi had actually been at her house when her daughter was alone. She stood and walked to the cabinet and reached for the vodka on the top shelf. "I need something a little stronger before I tell you the next part."

When the others eyeballed the half-empty bottle of vodka, there was a collective cheer around the table.

"Now you're talking," Lainey said, as she shoved her glass toward Maddy. "Hit me."

"Dammit!" Kate said. "Sometimes it sucks having a job where people's lives actually depend on you." She refilled her glass with juice only. "I have to say, Maddy, I'm getting a little nervous about why you need alcohol to tell us something. You hardly ever drink—and never before dinner."

Maddy poured a small amount of vodka into her juice and sat down with the manila folder she'd grabbed from the counter. After downing a big gulp, she opened it and slid the picture across the table.

"Oh my God!" Lainey was the first to react. "When was this taken?"

"A few days before Bernardi was arrested."

"What in the world was he doing at your house?" Deena asked, unable to hide the horrified look on her face. It was just the reaction Maddy had expected.

"He was looking for Alan Foxworthy. Thought the man lived here."

"Should that name ring a bell with us?" Kate asked.

Maddy blew out a breath. "He's the guy who fought with Bernardi at the bar—the one who was in the cell next to him and was also shot."

"What? That makes no sense," Lainey said. "And isn't he the guy who positively identified you as the shooter"

Maddy nodded. "I've racked my brain trying to figure out a reason why he'd say that. He was in on the plan to frame me or the person that shot him was disguised to look like me somehow. Either way, it would've been a lot easier to wait until Bernardi was out of jail before killing him."

Who took the picture? Tessa asked.

"I don't know. The cops found it in Bernardi's apartment when they searched it after he was killed," Maddy responded then remembered the others hadn't heard the question. "Tessa wanted to know who took the picture."

"Okay," Lainey said, shoving the photo back across the table. "Sounds like it's time we have a little chat with our mystery barfly."

"Already on it," Maddy said. "I have her address, and I thought I'd run over there this afternoon to see if she can shed some light on all this. Who's with me?"

"Can't," Kate said, scrunching her lips in a pout. "I always miss out on all the good stuff. Hope I make it all the way through my residency so these eighteen hour days will be worth it."

"I can't, either." Deena poured herself another screwdriver. "I'm working from home today so it doesn't count as a sick day."

Maddy made eye contact with Lainey as a huge grin flashed across her sister's face.

"I wouldn't miss it for the world. My curiosity is killing me. Besides, I need to bone up on my investigative skills. Anchoring the six o'clock news on the weekend doesn't exactly stimulate my journalistic mind." She looked around the table. "What about you, Tessa?"

Oh, hell yes. Seeing my two sisters go after that poor defenseless ho will make my day.

"It's settled then. Tessa's in, too. We'll plan on meeting back here again day after tomorrow and go from there. We'll report everything to you, Deena, so you can add it to the notes. That way, they'll be all together when—" Maddy stopped abruptly when the doorbell rang, nearly causing her to jump out of her skin.

Scrambling from her seat, she walked quickly to the door, wondering if the wallpaper samples she'd requested before this fiasco started had finally arrived. A lot of good they'd be to her now since there was no way she could afford any more improvements on the house.

"Have you checked my references yet?"

Up this close to Jake Matthews, Maddy noticed how blue his eyes were and how the nice citrusy smell from his body tickled her nostrils. "I've started, but I'm not finished yet," she lied.

Actually she'd had Tom Rogers do a complete criminal background check on him the day before. To her surprise Jake Matthews was an ex-cop who now worked for an insurance company that catered to the world's wealthiest clients, insuring all their high-dollar toys and assets.

"Didn't find any dirt on me, did you?" He leaned against the door frame, never once taking his eyes off her face.

"Not yet," she said, trying desperately to show him that his gaze didn't faze her. "If there's something there, trust me, I'll find it."

She met his stare with an intense one of her own, wondering how a decorated cop like him—according to Roger's information— could leave law enforcement altogether and be satisfied working for an insurance company.

And what exactly did an ex-cop do at an insurance company, anyhow?

Jake broke eye contact first then pulled out his wallet and handed her a check. "Like I said, I'll only be in town for a short time. Here's two thousand dollars for a couple of months rent plus an extra thousand as a security deposit. That should just about cover it for both rooms upstairs, right?"

Maddy stared at the check in his hand. It was way more than she'd ever intended to charge. More importantly, it was more than enough to reach the ten grand she needed for her lawyer's retainer fee. She wanted so badly to reach for it and have all her money problems go away for a while, but something held her back.

She cocked her head and narrowed her eyes at him. "Why'd you leave the San Antonio Police Department?" She didn't care if it was out of line and dangerously skirting the none-of-your-business range. If she was seriously considering letting this guy live in her house with her ten-year-old daughter, she had to know he wasn't a danger to them. "And don't lie to me because I'll find out soon enough."

His eyes flashed anger before a glint of mischief replaced it. "Been checking up on me down at the station, I see." He lowered his head and shifted the weight from one foot to the other before glancing back up at her, a look of sadness now on his face. "I lost my partner in a drug bust. After that I questioned why I was a cop. I became a liability to anybody who was unfortunate enough to partner with me." He took a deep breath then let it out slowly, sending the unmistakable whiff of alcohol her way.

Warning flags popped up in her head like weeds in a flower garden.

Chapter Fourteen

"You've been drinking," Maddy accused. "And it's not even noon yet."

"I could say the same thing about you," Jake fired back.

She slammed her hand over her mouth, remembering the two vodka screwdrivers she'd imbibed only moments before. He was right. Who was she to judge when she was guilty of the exact same thing she'd just chastised him for?

But she wasn't about to let him off the hook so easily.

"The difference is I'm not trying to rent a room where there's a minor child. The report on you says you have a drinking problem. I need to know if it's true."

He lifted his chin and stared her down. He was definitely nervous, and it was her experience that when someone was uncomfortable, there was usually a good reason why. She was pretty sure his had everything to do with alcohol.

"I won't have an alcoholic living in my house."

He nodded. "Fair enough. No drinking while I'm here. You can throw my sorry ass out—no questions asked— anytime you think I've fallen off the wagon. You can even keep all the rent money on top of the security deposit." He paused to study her face. "So will you at least consider renting me your upstairs rooms?"

Before she could respond, all three of her sisters rushed over to stand behind her.

"And you are?" Lainey asked, stepping in front of Maddy as if to protect her, a maneuver that didn't go unnoticed by Matthews.

His eyes crinkled and he held out his hand. "Jake Matthews. I'm trying to rent a room here for a few months."

As Lainey shook his hand, Maddy heard Kate's sharp intake of breath when she stepped forward and got her first look at the ex-cop.

"Kate Garcia, Maddy's youngest sister," she said, emphasizing the youngest part.

"I'm Deena Hernandez, also her younger sister." She made a sweeping motion with her arm. "Come on in, and we'll talk about it."

I hate being dead, Tessa said, standing so close to Jake it was a wonder he didn't feel a chill. *This guy is freaking gorgeous. I'm suddenly reminded that sex is like air. It's only important if you're not getting any.*

Maddy held out her arm to stop Jake from coming in. She wasn't ready to deal with it yet, not with all the other things on her mind. "My sisters were just leaving. I have your card, Mr. Matthews. I'll be making a decision sometime today, and I'll call you."

She closed the door quickly before she changed her mind. The check in his hand was too tempting, and she had to really give it some thought. Her decision would be more rational if she made it away from those searing blue eyes.

"Are you nuts?" Deena asked. "Aren't you desperate for money? You're turning away a guy who wants to pay to use the rooms upstairs for a few months—the rooms that are currently vacant, I might add? The least you can do is check him out."

"I already have," Maddy said, nudging her sisters back into the kitchen. "He's an ex-cop."

"That's perfect," Lainey said. "Not only will you have extra money but the guy looks like he could hold his own in case someone decides to pay you a little visit." She picked up the picture of Bernardi and Jessie and pointed at the dead guy. "Need I say more?"

"I know," Maddy said. "And I'm considering it, but I want to mull it over a little while longer. It's a big decision to open up your house up a perfect stranger."

"Want me to get Colt to vet him?" Lainey asked.

"What? No," Maddy responded quickly. "Rogers has already started the process. Besides, you'd have to admit to Colt that you were over here when you met him, and you and I both know your husband would see right through that. Then the nonstop lectures about us butting out of his investigation would commence."

Lainey slapped her hand to her head. "Oh dear God, yes. I forgot about that. Tom Rogers can do it just as easily as Colt."

"Well, guys, I hate to break up this party, but I really do have to run. I'm already late," Kate said, grabbing her purse and heading for the door.

"Me too," Deena said, following her. "And make sure you call Kate and me the minute you two get back from the bar girl's house. Then we'll meet in a few days and plan our next move."

When Lainey and Maddy were finally alone, Lainey asked, "Have you heard any more from your lawyer?"

Maddy shook her head. "Only that he's coming up Friday with some of his team to discuss my case." She swallowed. "He'll need the retainer then."

"Do you have it?"

"Most of it."

Maddy thought about how many problems would be resolved if she just allowed Jake Matthews to rent her upstairs. What could it hurt? Rogers had already done a thorough background check and had all but confirmed there were no problems. Other than the fact that he'd left his job a year ago, possibly because of his drinking. Most importantly, nothing in his history indicated the slightest hint of issues with young girls. Jessie might even be safer with him around.

But what worried her most at the moment, if she closed her eyes right now, she knew she would still see him standing at her doorstep. She could visualize his light blue shirt opened at the neck just enough to allow a peek at the few chest hairs poking through, the faded blue jeans that looked like they were made especially for him. Even though she knew Lainey was right about having him around for protection, the fact that she was even thinking about stuff like that scared the crap out of her.

She was jarred from her thoughts when her phone rang, causing her to gasp. After glancing at caller ID, she made a face at Lainey before answering. "Hey, Colt, what's up? Tell me you have good news."

She hoped he didn't pick up on the guilt in her voice for sneaking around behind his back. Knowing her brother-in-law the way she did, he probably would. She braced herself for his reprimand.

"I'm at the hospital with Flanagan," he said before muttering to someone else, "Don't let anyone in that room until after forensics gets here." There was a slight pause before he continued talking to her. "Sorry, Maddy, I'll make this quick because I have a lot of things to do before—"

"You're at the hospital?" Maddy interrupted. "Is everything okay?" Silently she prayed that it was. After receiving a call a few years back telling her that Jessie had fallen and broken her arm at school, she now dreaded it whenever someone called from there.

"Foxworthy's dead."

"What? I thought he was getting better."

"He was," Colt said. "But if my gut is correct, someone decided to hasten his demise."

"You're saying he was murdered?"

"We won't know that until we get the autopsy report, but it looks like a hospital employee may have been involved." He paused. "Gotta go. There's the ME now. I'll call when I have more information."

Maddy disconnected, her mind racing with all the possibilities about who would have killed the man who had positively IDed her as Bernardi's killer and thanking her lucky stars that she was nowhere near the place when it happened.

"What did he say?" Lainey's face twisted with concern. "You look like you've seen a ghost." Her gaze shifted upward. "Sorry, Tessa."

"He's at the hospital. He thinks someone killed Alan Foxworthy."

As much as I'd like to say I'm sorry to hear that, Tessa said, *I can't. It means they won't be able to use his testimony. This calls for another drink, sis. It just might be the best news we've heard since that scumbag Bernardi took a bullet to his head.*

* * * * *

He drove past her house just as two women exited and made their way to the cars parked out front, whistling under his breath when he got a closer look at the one who looked younger. Dressed in green scrubs that didn't hide the outline of a hot little body underneath, she wore her dark hair pulled back in a ponytail, making her look like an innocent schoolgirl. He felt a familiar stirring below the belt. Even though the last thing he needed was to be noticed, he took his foot off the gas pedal and slowed for a better look.

"Caramba!" He muttered under his breath.

She looked to be in her middle twenties, and although he usually didn't go for chicks that much younger than him, he would definitely make an exception in her case.

His eyes moved to the other woman, and instantly, he decided this one wasn't his type. Her hair was disheveled and she could stand to lose at least fifteen pounds. A closer look at her face left no doubt she was the cop's sister, and he guessed the looker walking beside her was, as well.

He remembered the first time he'd seen a picture of Madelyn Castillo and thought what a waste of a gorgeous female. It was a crying shame she'd have to rot in a jail somewhere, although he was sure there would be a lot of happy inmates when the prison bus pulled up and the lady felons got their first look at her. Just thinking about it warmed his insides—as well as a few other places.

But sending the cop to jail had never been his intention. He figured with her being a police officer and her brother-in-law as the town sheriff, more than likely she wouldn't see jail time. A slap on the wrist or even probation with community service maybe, but he hadn't thought they'd actually prosecute her for killing a douche bag like Bernardi.

After making a U-turn at the end of the block, he eased the car to the curb and waited until both cars were gone before driving back up the street past Castillo's house. Deciding there was nothing more to see, he turned left at the stop sign, glancing one last time over his shoulder at the cop's house in time to spot two more women coming down the sidewalk. Although he was too far away to be a hundred percent certain, it looked like one of the ladies might be the cop herself.

His curiosity piqued, he decided he had nothing better to do before heading back to Dallas, and he pulled over into a discreet spot where he watched the women climb into an SUV and head his way. Ducking down low enough so he wouldn't be noticed, he waited until they passed, then quickly turned around and followed. In case either of them had noticed his car passing the house earlier, he kept three cars between his black Land Rover and the SUV. So far everything had gone as planned. The last thing he needed now was to arouse the cop's suspicions.

He had no idea where they were going, but he decided it wouldn't hurt to tag along. If they ended up at the nail salon, so be it. But his gut told him they weren't hightailing it to a day of pampering.

He turned south when they did, sneaking a peek at his GPS on the dashboard. They were heading toward the airport.

About that time his cell phone blared, and he reached down to check caller ID. His mother! No way he was in the mood to listen to her cry again about how much she missed Junior. The woman would never get it through her head that her youngest son had been a loser all his life—and that if it wasn't for him, Junior would have ended up in jail or worse long before his disappearance.

He'd hoped with Junior out of the way, his mother would turn to him for comfort, would change the way she felt about him. But Junior had been gone for over two weeks now, and the old woman still cried every night.

No, her feelings toward him would never change, and he might as well accept that fact. No matter how hard he tried, there was never any love left over for him. In his heart he knew there never would be, yet he continually strived for her approval.

What was it they said about insanity? Doing the same thing over and over again, expecting a different result. That about summed up his relationship with his mother.

He knew it was crazy, but the little boy in him still wanted her to look him in the eye and tell him she loved him. He ran the biggest drug ring in North Texas, had some of the most powerful men in the city asking how high when he said jump, and yet, he was still trying to get his mother's praise.

Pathetic!

But for now, he'd let her believe Junior was coming home, that this time was no different than his many other episodes where he'd stay away as long as two months without any communication at all. Usually when that happened, there were drugs involved. Less than six months ago he'd found Junior holed up in some shit-shack in Juárez with a toothless Hispanic woman who fed his heroin habit. He'd lost a huge amount of time and money looking for him.

But there would be no money or time lost now. Not because he was sick of always having to save his older brother, but because he knew exactly where Junior was. His brother had screwed up for the last time and now lay at the bottom of Lake Lewisville tied to a couple of concrete blocks. No way he wanted his mother to know that.

His attention was diverted when the cop and the other woman turned down the street into an old neighborhood outside city limits. When they stopped at a small house that looked like it was condemned—and if not, should be--he pulled over farther down the road. Reaching in the glove compartment he grabbed his binoculars and trained them on the two women now marching up the sidewalk.

* * * * *

Surveying the rundown house, Maddy took a deep breath. If all went well, they'd leave with a better understanding of what actually went down at Cowboys Galore the night Bernardi was killed. How they would get that information out of Chrissy Rockford was left to be seen. They would just play it by ear.

Climbing out of the car, they walked up a sidewalk in desperate need of attention. The concrete was full of cracks, some running the entire length of the walkway and most if it crumbled so badly, they had to step into the grass to get past. The yard itself lacked anything resembling color and the weeds were almost as tall as a healthy toddler. If this was any indication of Chrissy Rockford's gardening skills, the woman obviously did not have a green thumb.

"Hope this isn't poison ivy," Lainey said, hopping over a huge clump of weeds. "I am so in trouble if it is."

"I don't think it is. But just in case, do you want to sit in the car while I have a little chat with our mystery bar girl?"

Lainey shook her head. "No way. We're in this together, remember? There's always Benadryl if I start to itch."

They walked up the dilapidated steps and knocked on the door several times. After a few minutes, Maddy was ready to give up, figuring either the house was vacant or Chrissy Rockford wasn't there. She was about to turn away when a voice came out of nowhere.

"Are you the people from the insurance company?"

Both Maddy and Lainey jumped as a rotund older woman in a shabby dress with an apron covered in flour, suddenly appeared on the bottom step.

"I'm Abilene Witherspoon," the woman explained when she saw their reaction. "I didn't mean to frighten you. Thought you might be the people from the insurance company. Chrissy said she couldn't wait here any longer and asked me to give you this."

She handed a folded piece of paper to Maddy, who glanced up at Lainey and arched an eyebrow. They probably should've mentioned they weren't insurance agents looking for Chrissy, but the note was too tempting.

Why would Chrissy be talking to an insurance agent in the first place? Insurance for what?

She unfolded the note and read it before looking up at the neighbor. "Thanks, Mrs. Witherspoon. We'll catch up with her there." She started to leave then stopped. Pulling out a picture of Bernardi, she handed it to the woman. "Ever seen this guy over here?"

The neighbor studied it for a minute. "I can't be certain, but he looks like he might be the one I've seen picking Chrissy up on several occasions. Does he drive a Caddy?"

Maddy shrugged. "That I don't know. Did Chrissy ever tell you about any the guys she dated?"

"Not really, although she mentioned the other day that her life was about to change soon. Something about a necklace being the answer to her prayers."

"A necklace?"

"Yeah, she never really told me what she meant by that." The woman turned. "Well, I've got to go and finish making my pies crusts for the church bake sale this week. It was nice talking to you."

"Same here," Lainey followed Maddy back to the car. When they were inside she turned on the ignition and eased away from the curb. "Come on, Maddy. I'm dying here. What did the note say?"

But Maddy wasn't paying attention. Instead, she was digging through the bag she'd brought and smiled as she pulled out several manila folders. Opening them one at a time, she finally found what she was looking for.

"Ah ha! I knew it!"

"Knew what? Dammit, Maddy, I'm going to wreck this car trying to see what you're looking at. And by the way, where are we going?"

Maddy grinned. "Sorry." She opened the note Mrs. Witherspoon had given her. "It says Chrissy will be at 219 Fairview Avenue all day today."

"So what's the big deal about that?"

Maddy hitched her eyebrows a couple of times then grinned. "If memory serves, that's the newer part of Vineyard over by the town square dominated by condos and townhouses. Heard the cheapest one goes for two hundred grand." She pointed to the file in her hand. "Says here Bernardi lived in that part of town. Want to guess the address of his condo?"

"No way!" Lainey pushed down on the gas pedal. "We have to get there before Chrissy decides to leave. It will be hard for her to lie about the relationship Bernardi claimed to have with her if she's at his house right now."

My thoughts exactly.

Maddy twirled around to see Tessa in the back seat rubbing her hands together.

I live for shit like this. She frowned. *Oh wait! I forgot I'm dead. Bummer.*

"It's about time you got here," Maddy said. "We need you to snoop around while we keep Chrissy occupied."

That's one of my all-time favorite things to do. Thought you'd never ask. She settled into the leather seat. *And tell Lainey she'd better stop at WalMart and pick up some cortisone cream. That was poison ivy back there.*

Chapter Fifteen

"**W**ow! I thought you said this guy ran a small business," Lainey said as they waited outside the townhouse.

"He did." Maddy looked around. "He contracted with several businesses in the area and did their payroll." She whistled. "I'm in the wrong business, for sure."

Hundred bucks says he was making book or doing something illegal to supplement his income. Tessa moved closer to the door and looked into the peep hole.

"Do you see anything?" Maddy asked, anxious to get this over with and head back home. Then she remembered that Jessie was at the aquarium and wouldn't be back until after five. She took a deep breath to relax. Staying calm was key if they were going to pull this off.

Everyone knows you can't see through these from the outside, Maddy. Tessa laughed. *Unfortunately, being dead doesn't give me super powers.*

Just then the door opened, and they got their first look at Chrissy Rockford. Standing about five-feet eight, she was wearing tight black leggings and an oversized sweatshirt. The mysterious bar girl, who in all probablility earned her keep by taking money for her sexual services, could have passed for the girl next-door. Her long blond hair was pulled back and secured with a clip, a style that highlighted her high cheekbones and green-blue eyes.

Damn! No wonder men paid to tickle her fancy and have her tickle theirs back. Tessa slipped past her and went inside.

"Ms. Rockford, we're from the insurance company," Lainey said, extending her hand. "May we come in?"

Maddy coughed to cover her surprise. She had no idea her sister was going to try something like this, but it was a great ploy. No doubt the woman would slam the door in their faces if she knew Maddy was the one accused of killing her boyfriend.

Well I'll be damned! Goody-two-shoes Lainey knows how to lie. I am so proud at this moment.

Chrissy opened the door wider and motioned for them to come in. Once the door shut behind her, Maddy surveyed the living room to the left. Decorated with a humongous gold and brown couch that had probably seen a lot of action, the room reeked of bad taste, right down to the semi-pornographic, 3-D picture of two women and a man framing half of one wall. A large flat screen TV hung on the opposite one.

"Please, have a seat," Chrissy said. "Pardon the mess. This is my boyfriend's house and he's been overseas on a trip this past week."

Yeah, right. More like in a drawer at the morgue. Tessa plopped down on the brown couch. *Most men prefer the rustic look. This dude went for ugly.*

"No problem," Maddy said, picking up a newspaper from an identically-upholstered chair opposite the couch, and sitting down.

"I'm surprised to see two women show up," Chrissy said, settling in nearly on top of Tessa, who scooted away in the nick of time.

"Why's that?" Lainey asked.

"Well, when I got the call about the necklace, the man said he would be stopping by."

At the mention of the necklace both Maddy and Laney shot up straighter. Was this the necklace Mrs. Witherspoon had told them about? The one that Chrissy said would change her life?

"He's our supervisor," Maddy lied. "Something came up at the office, and since we're all familiar with the case, he sent us to do the preliminary paperwork." She reached in the bag with all her police files and pulled one out, opening it and pretending to read it. She glanced back up at Chrissy. "Now tell us again about the necklace."

Chrissy narrowed her eyes, and for a minute, Maddy worried that she was on to them. Then she slid further back on the couch and took a deep breath. "All I know is what Gino told me."

"Gino?" Maddy decided to play dumb.

"He was..." She caught herself and smiled up at them before continuing, "He *is* my boyfriend. He's out of the country on business, remember?" Chrissy shifted uncomfortably. "Your boss assured me that I would collect a finder's fee. Nothing's changed, has it??"

"Absolutely not," Lainey assured her. "And what was the last amount our representative quoted you?"

"Two hundred thousand."

Maddy caught herself before she gasped. It must be some kind of necklace to rake in that kind of finder's fee. Somebody obviously really wanted it back. She wondered if that was reason enough to kill for it.

"We've been authorized to raise that amount another fifty thousand dollars," Lainey said, smiling so sweetly at Chrissy that Maddy thought her face would crack.

Chrissy beamed at the mention of more money and nodded her approval.

I almost feel sorry for this broad with both of you working her like a tag team. Tessa stood up. *I'm going to do my sneaking around while you guys continue to lie like hell.* She disappeared down the hallway in the obvious direction of the bedroom.

"All we have to do is work out the details," Maddy said fueling Lainey's lie.

"Like I told your boss, I'm pretty sure Gino has it in a safety deposit box, and as soon as I get my hands on it, I'll give your office a call. I don't expect that to take long."

"Does Gino know about you getting the finder's fee?"

A frightened look crossed Chrissy's face. "No. That's why I want to get this over with quickly before he gets back from his trip. I found the key hidden in the freezer, and as I said, I'm confident I'll find the necklace when I go to the bank tomorrow morning."

"Have you personally seen this necklace?" Maddy asked, thinking it would be a lot easier to run a trace on a stolen piece of jewelry if they had a description.

Chrissy shook her head. "Gino guarded it like a pit bull in a junkyard. He only mentioned it to me when I heard him talking about it one night on the phone. Said he was going overseas to sell it, and when he got back, he'd be able to live the high life like he used to."

"Aren't you worried about what he'll do when he finds out what you've done?" Maddy asked, wishing she could tell her to cut the bull—that they all knew the only trip Gino would be taking anytime soon was down south, and she wasn't referring to Mexico.

"That's really none of your business," Chrissy said. For a minute Maddy was sure she'd blown it before the woman's face softened and she continued, "Like I told your boss, Gino has already made contact with a French jeweler as well as one in Saudi Arabia. Both are itching to get their hands on the necklace. He was supposedly going to meet the Saudi one day this week before he..." She stopped suddenly, and Maddy knew she'd been this close to saying before he was killed.

Bingo! Tessa said, running into the room, excitement all over her face. *Her purse is on the bed with half the contents thrown around as if she was digging for something before we arrived. There are pictures of her with other men and a book opened to a page with the names of some high-profile Dallas politicians that you have to see, Maddy. Our Chrissy is not Little Miss Innocence Personified as she's trying to make us believe.*

Maddy made eye contact with Lainey and nodded. The plan was if Tessa found anything, she'd check it out while Lainey kept Chrissy talking in the living room. Maddy hoped it would work. Standing, she asked, "Do you mind if I use the restroom? I've had way too much coffee today."

"Down the hall. First door on the left." Chrissy pointed in that direction.

"So, as soon as you have the necklace in your possession, we'll be by with the check," Lainey said, doing her part keeping Chrissy occupied. "Both our boss and the client will be very happy to hear this."

"The sooner I can put this all behind me, the better," Chrissy said. Then as if she suddenly remembered her manners, she said, "There's cold beer and bottled water in the fridge. Can I get you something?" She started to get up before Lainey thrust out her arm and stopped her.

"Oh gosh, no, but thanks. I would like to ask you about what kind of moisturizer you use, though. Your skin is absolutely amazing."

Maddy stopped in her tracks halfway to the bedroom when she realized that Chrissy was about to get up and go to the kitchen for beverages. But after hearing her sister's excellent maneuver to keep the woman talking, she breathed a sigh of relief and continued to the bedroom. The minute she walked in she spotted Tessa sanding beside the biggest circular bed she'd ever seen, elevated on a platform under a mirrored ceiling.

Jeez! Bernardi really was a sleaze.

Look at the pictures, Tessa said excitedly. *If we weren't sure before, we are now. This girl was definitely turning tricks.*

Maddy moved to the bed and stared at the photos. Her hand was shaking as she reached for one and stared down at the picture of Chrissy in bed with an unknown man in a very compromising position. A closer look showed the guy with his eyes closed, just lying there while Chrissy performed for the camera.

"Oh my God!" she whispered, flipping through the other pictures. "Why would Chrissy have pictures of her with all these guys? And who was operating the camera? Could she and Bernardi have been running a blackmail scam on married men?"

You have to admit it would be a great reason for one of them to kill the dirtbag, Tessa said, obviously proud of herself for finding the pictures.

Maddy spread the photos around on the bed and leaned closer. There were five pictures in all and every one of them was basically the same pose—Chrissy performing oral sex on each man. And in every photo, the guys looked like they were asleep. Probably drugged. Maddy pulled out her phone and snapped a shot of all five.

Then she grabbed one and brought it closer to her face for a better look. Something was very familiar about the guy in the last photo. What was it?

What do you see, sis? Tessa asked, moving closer. *'Cause all I see is a dude with the smallest piece of equipment in the history of blow jobs. This is one sailor who learned the hard way about the three knots.*

"Three knots?"

Knot hard, knot in, and knot getting his money back.

Maddy started to grin before she gasped and her eyes widened. "Holy crap!"

What?

"It's Alan Foxworthy," Maddy said, unable to contain the excitement in her voice. "He's the guy who was in the cell next to Bernardi and who positively identified me as her killer. The guy who was probably murdered just today while he lay in his hospital bed."

So?

"Don't you get it? All along we've assumed the bar fight was between two strangers and now this proves they knew each other. Or at least Chrissy and Foxworthy did. And although Foxworthy may have not known Bernardi per se, I'll bet Bernardi was behind the camera when these were taken and recognized him that night at the bar. That may explain why fists were flying. If Foxworthy was being blackmailed it stands to reason he might have confronted Chrissy and Bernardi at the bar."

So why'd he grab Chrissy's ass?

"I have no idea." Maddy snapped one more shot of Chrissy and Foxworthy before she arranged the pictures back on the bed just the way she'd found them. "Come on." She motioned for Tessa to follow. "We've got to sit down and figure out what this all means."

Wait.

Maddy stopped in her tracks and pivoted to face her sister again. "What?"

Look at this. You won't believe it.

Maddy focused her attention on the small black notebook that Tessa was pointing to and immediately spotted the name of a congressman from Westgate, a wealthy suburb north of Dallas. She grabbed it and flipped to a random page and gasped.

Tell me it's something that will help you, Tessa said, inching closer until she was nearly on top of Maddy.

"I see the names of a lot of pretty powerful men in here." She turned the page. "Holy cow! Here's the current deputy mayor of Dallas." She whistled under her breath. "What if Bernardi and Chrissy were blackmailing more than just the out-of-towners who cheated on their wives? What if they had a slew of politicians and influential people contributing to their payroll every month?"

That would be one helluva motive to kill the SOB, don't ya think? Tessa jumped up and squealed, visibly excited that she'd been the one to find the book.

Maddy thought she heard a sound in the hallway and quickly stuck the book down her bra. "Colt will kill me, but I'm taking this for now," she said when Tessa scrunched her eyebrows. "Come on. We need to get out of here before Chrissy gets suspicious and comes looking for us."

After walking back into the living room, she meandered over to the door, signaling with a swipe across her neck for Lainey to wrap things up and end the conversation.

"Well, Chrissy, we'll be in touch," Lainey said rising from the couch. "Call the office as soon as you have the necklace in your possession." She headed for the door, talking over her shoulder. "Don't get up. We'll see ourselves out."

When they were settled in the car, Maddy turned to her. "You won't believe what Tessa found?" She pulled out her phone and showed Lainey the pictures.

"Other than proof that Chrissy gives head, probably for money, so what? Didn't we already suspect that?"

"Yeah, but we had no idea one of her johns was Alan Foxworthy." She enlarged the picture before shoving it toward Lainey.

"So they did know each other. Should we tell Colt about this?"

A look of panic crossed Maddy's face. "And how are we going to explain how we found out?" She shook her head. "My instincts tell me that Colt already knows. We need to organize another sister meeting to figure out what this all means and what we should do next."

"What about the necklace? How does that fit in?"

"I have no idea, Lainey, and right now I'm too excited to even think straight." Maddy took a deep breath and blew it out slowly. "And there's more." Quickly, she filled her sister in about the black book they'd found in Chrissy's purse.

"What's it all mean?"

"I don't know, but it's looking more and more like I might be able to get off on a reasonable doubt defense."

She couldn't wait to tell her lawyer. Thinking about Tony Pirelli reminded her that she still didn't have the full retainer he was expecting when he came to Vineyard on Friday.

Taking the money from Jake Matthews was looking more and more likely every minute, especially with this new evidence that could have her back at her old job soon.

An idea suddenly popped into her head. "What are you doing tomorrow morning?"

Lainey shrugged. "Nothing exciting. Why?" She narrowed her eyes. "I know that look, Maddy, and I have to say I'm pretty freaking excited about hearing what you have up your sleeve."

"Stop by Mickey D's in the morning after Colt leaves for the station and Gracie is on her way to school. Pick up a couple of Egg McMuffins and some coffee then come and get me."

"This is getting good," Lainey said, rubbing her hands together. "Where are we going?"

"On a stake-out to see why this necklace is causing such a fuss."

* * * * *

He parked close enough to watch as the two women walked up to a townhouse in a really nice neighborhood that was a far cry from the one they'd just left. Reaching for the binoculars for a better look, he focused first on the cop's backside and was about to check out the second woman's ass when he caught a glimpse of the blond standing inside the house.

There was something familiar about her, but he couldn't quite put his finger on it. He waited about fifteen minutes after the women went into the house before deciding there was nothing more to see. Pulling away from the curb, he headed for the Interstate. Halfway to Dallas, it hit him.

He knew exactly why the blonde had looked so familiar.

Chapter Sixteen

Maddy waved goodbye to her daughter the next day as the school bus pulled away from the curb. Glancing impatiently at her watch for the third time in as many minutes, she blew out a breath. Today she and Lainey were going to sit in the car and follow Chrissy Rockford when she went to the bank to open Gino Bernardi's safety deposit box. The woman was counting on finding the infamous necklace that was supposed to change her life—the necklace that very well might be just what Maddy's lawyer needed to get her off the hook for Bernardi's murder.

Maddy had no idea if it really would be useful in her defense—or as a possible motive for killing the man—but right now it was the only lead she had. If nothing else, she'd get to spend the day with her sister and even get a free breakfast out of the deal. Even though it had only been less than a week since she'd been accused of murder and put on paid administrative leave, she was going stir-crazy cooped up in the house all day.

When the doorbell rang, she headed that way, grabbing her purse, sweater, and the bag containing all the files relating to her case. Her mouth began to water with thoughts of breakfast, much like Pavlov's dog did at the sound of the bell. But that old dog never had an Egg McMuffin with his name on it like she did.

Her smile faded when she saw that it wasn't Lainey standing on her porch.

"Going somewhere?" Jake Matthews leaned against the doorjamb and didn't even try to keep his eyes on her face as they roamed up her entire body.

For a second, she wished she had worn something more feminine than sweatpants and a long-sleeved T-shirt, but she quickly dispelled that notion. She was about to go on a stakeout, for God's sake, not a date.

"Matter of fact I am," she replied, meeting his stare with one of her own. "I thought you were my sister."

"Have you given any more thought to renting me your upstairs rooms?"

He was standing close enough for her to smell the faint odor of citrus. She took a step backward to put more space between them. At least it wasn't alcohol she smelled.

She arched her brow. "Let me make sure we both understand the terms. You want to live upstairs for two months, and you swear there will be no drinking in the house while you're here, am I correct?"

He shifted uncomfortably. "No alcohol in this house ever, and if I decide to have a few drinks out, I'll check into a hotel for the night. Agreed?"

She pondered that for a minute before remembering that her lawyer was driving back to Vineyard in two days and was expecting her to hand over his full ten-thousand dollar retainer—which she did not have at the moment. The man was ready to place a three-thousand dollar check in her hand, which would be more than enough for her defense.

What would it hurt to have him upstairs? She'd insist there be no interaction alone with her daughter, plus Rogers had called last night to tell her he was finished with the background check he'd done on Matthews. Other than the possible drinking problem, her partner had only found citations for bravery and community service awards. Besides, Jake had already assured her that if she caught him drinking in the house, she could throw him out on his behind and keep the balance of the check.

She needed to get that in writing.

And the man was a trained cop—and a very good one, according to Rogers. It might be nice knowing there was someone around to fight off a bad guy or two.

"I can live with that as long as you don't come into this house drunk as a skunk," she informed him. "And no bringing women into my house either. I do have a child to consider."

"Agreed on both counts. So, is it a deal?" When she nodded, he reached into his shirt pocket and pulled out the check. "It's all here."

"When do you want to move in?"

"What about now? I've already checked out of the hotel and everything I have is in my car."

She was hoping she could put him off until the next day, but spotting Lainey's car pulling into the driveway, she didn't have time to argue with him. Snapping her own house key off her key ring, she handed it to him. "Lock up when you're finished, and put this under the mat. It's the only one I have until I can get another one made at the hardware store." She handed it to him just as Lainey walked up the sidewalk.

"Hello, Mr. Matthews. It's nice to see you again," she said before turning to Maddy. "Are you ready? I've got the food and drinks in the car?"

"Where are you ladies off to?" Jake asked, unable to hide the curiosity in his eyes.

"Nowhere," Maddy blurted.

"Actually, we're spending a sister day together," Lainey said. "You know, pedicures, shopping...all the usual stuff girls do when their kids are in school."

"So why do you need to take food and drinks?"

Maddy stole a quick glance toward Lainey. "Not that it's any of your business, but we go to the park for lunch when the weather is predicted to be as beautiful as it is today." She wondered why he was asking. The niggling thought that maybe she'd been a little too quick opening her home to the ex-cop, now insurance agent, wouldn't go away.

Insurance agent? Maybe he could clear up something that had been bothering her ever since they'd left Chrissy Rockford's house the day before. She took a deep breath and proceeded, "Let me ask you something, Mr. Matthews—"

"Call me Jake," he interrupted. "I think the fact that I will be living in your house meets the qualification for using first names, don't you?"

Something about the way his eyes crinkled sent a rush of heat up her cheeks. "Agreed. I'm Maddy. Now back to my question. Why would an insurance company pay someone a lot of money for a finder's fee? I mean, if a claim had already been paid for something that was lost and later found, why would they hand over more money to someone who may very well have been responsible for the item going missing in the first place?"

The amusement in his eyes disappeared, replaced by a scowl. "Why are you asking?"

"No reason," Lainey answered before grabbing Maddy's arm. "We have to go, Jake. Maybe I'll see you around." She took a step forward but he never budged.

"Guess you haven't heard. I live here now." He pivoted and walked to his car.

As he opened the trunk and pulled out a small suitcase, Maddy caught her breath and followed Lainey out the door. "Don't even ask," she said. "And get the food. We're taking my car in case Chrissy remembers yours from yesterday."

After piling into Maddy's Honda, they headed down the road just as Jake Matthews shut the car trunk and walked up the sidewalk.

"That boy does have a nice back view," Lainey observed, finally twisting around to face forward. "Okay, should we go to Bernardi's apartment or to the shack Chrissy lives in?" She dug into the bag and pulled out a breakfast sandwich. After unwrapping it, she handed it to Maddy before grabbing one of her own.

"I asked Rogers to check on Bernardi's house right before you showed up. He said there's no one there. Apparently Chrissy's gone back to her own place."

They drove the rest of the way devouring the food and making small talk. As they turned down the familiar street, the first thing Maddy noticed was how deserted it was. Even though it was a school day, usually a neighborhood had some kind of action going on—a woman pushing a stroller, a mailman making deliveries. Something.

Maddy pulled up to the curb two doors away from Chrissy's house and turned off the engine. "Now comes the boring part where we sit back and wait." She pulled out the latest woman's magazine she'd picked up the other day at the supermarket. "You keep your eye on the house while I skim through this, then I'll take over while you check it out."

"It always looks like so much fun on the cop shows," Lainey said, leaning to her left to read with Maddy. "Jeez! What was Rebecca Lawrence thinking when she wore that dress?" She straightened back up when Maddy shot her a stern look. "Oh, sorry. Forgot I was supposed to be watching the house."

Some kennels don't have mirrors, Tessa said, suddenly appearing in the back seat. ***Anything happening yet?***

Maddy waved a greeting, and then shook her head. "We've only been here about ten minutes, but since the bank doesn't open for another half-hour it's a pretty safe bet she's still in there, probably getting a shower now."

"Hey, Tessa," Lainey said when she realized that Maddy wasn't talking to herself.

Hey, sis.

"She says hi," Maddy said, thinking it was so nice to see her sisters no longer at war like they'd been for nine years.

Guess when Lainey had helped Tessa solve her own murder, it had ended the rift. That and the fact that Lainey was now married to Tessa's ex.

She closed the magazine. "Since the three of us are together, now's as good a time as any to talk about Deena. Have either of you noticed a change in her lately?"

If by that you mean the way she's apparently eaten herself into way bigger clothes, then yes. I hate to see that happening to her. Mike is far from the perfect husband, but he has to notice, too.

"Something's bothering her," Lainey said. "Remember when I told her I'd seen Mike playing nice with another woman in Ruby's one day before they got married? She didn't believe me. Said I was reading too much into a casual lunch with a coworker. Then she went into a state of depression for two weeks."

You think he's found another playmate?

"Yeah, the louse hasn't changed, I'm afraid." Maddy said. "Deena told me the other day that he was working a lot of overtime at the lumberyard. I never said anything, but I happen to know firsthand that they've cut back over there because of the economy. Mike is lucky to still be working forty hours, let alone overtime."

He's a pig! Tessa said, scrunching her nose. *Deena has always been way too good for him. Some people are has-beens. Mike Hernandez is a never was.*

"That's the truth," Maddy said. "I'm not sure if I should approach her about this or wait until she's ready to talk about it. My guess is she wouldn't believe me even if I brought it up."

Men can be such assholes. I've always said if it has tires or testicles, it's gonna give you trouble.

Just then Maddy spied Mrs. Witherspoon skirting the weeds in Chrissy's yard and walking across the sidewalk to the steps. She grabbed the binoculars and focused on the woman.

Isn't that the neighbor lady from yesterday? Tessa asked. *I sure would like to get my hands on one of her pies right now. I'm starving. Even though I can't eat any, just smelling it would help.*

"Yeah, that's her. Wonder why Chrissy isn't answering?" Maddy handed the binoculars to Lainey.

After a few minutes, Mrs. Witherspoon apparently gave up and walked back down the steps. She disappeared into her own house.

"That's weird," Maddy said. "Why didn't Chrissy open the door? Think we might've missed her?"

"It's a possibility, but I doubt it. She seems like the kind of girl who stays up late and sleeps in. We were here at eight forty-five," Lainey said, setting the binoculars on the seat beside her and reaching in the bag for a Raspberry Petite Pastry.

"You're probably right." Maddy glanced at her watch. "But it's already after ten. As anxious as Chrissy was to get the finder's fee for the mystery necklace and get out of Dodge, I find it hard to believe she'd sleep in today."

"I say we give her another fifteen minutes and then go knock on the door," Lainey said.

"Okay. Got another one of those?" Maddy was already fumbling in the sack. When she found one, she took a big bite and leaned back against the headrest.

It was looking more and more like this was probably going to turn out to be a wasted morning. Had Chrissy left before the crack of dawn? Or was it possible she'd already found herself another camera-ready partner in crime and had spent the night on a sleepover.

Fifteen minutes seemed to take forever as they waited without much conversation. Finally, Maddy opened the door. "Let's go see if our girl is there. I'll leave it up to you, Lainey, to come up with a good reason why we're here if she does open the door. You seem to have a knack for thinking on your feet."

Lainey was already out of the car and caught up to Maddy. "I kind of do, don't I?" She huffed. "Watch and learn, big sister."

They maneuvered their way around the weeds and up the front steps where Maddy rang the doorbell. After a few minutes, she knocked on the door and was surprised when it opened slightly.

"What's up with that?" Lainey asked.

"Should we?"

Lainey swallowed. "Do you have your gun?" When Maddy shook her head, Lainey narrowed her eyes. "What can it hurt? If we get caught we'll just say we thought we heard her say, 'Come on in.'"

Maddy pushed the door the rest of the way open and shouted Chrissy's name several times. No response. After only two steps into the rundown house, the fine hairs on the back of her neck stood at attention. The place looked like an F-5 tornado had blown through. The dingy cushions on the upholstered couch were slit open with the padding strewn about, chairs were overturned, and a small TV was smashed on the floor.

Whatever happened here can't be good, Tessa said. **Somebody was seriously looking for something.**

Maddy made her way to the kitchen where most of the contents of the cabinets were laying on the counters and all over the floor. She noticed Chrissy's purse next to the toaster with all the contents dumped out.

A wave of apprehension swept over her, especially when she recognized most of the things from the purse except for one. The rubber-banded pictures of the five men having sex with Chrissy—the ones that she and Tessa had seen in the purse yesterday—were gone. She gave it a second look to make sure, but they weren't there. Could Chrissy have taken them out and put them in another hiding place? Or was it possible that they were the reason Chrissy's house had been tossed?

She looked up and made eye contact with Lainey whose body language said she was more than a little nervous, too.

"I'm going back to the bedroom," she said, hoping her voice didn't give away how frightened she was about doing that. "You stay here with Tessa."

She had no idea what she'd find there—hopefully, nothing—but she wanted to make sure Lainey wasn't traumatized by something gruesome. She chided herself for letting her imagination get the best of her. Chrissy was probably having breakfast in bed at some hotel after a night of partying.

She opened the bedroom door slowly, immediately noticing that the queen-size bed was empty and the comforter and pillows were all over the floor. Cautiously, she walked closer, her breath coming faster with each step.

When she was close enough to touch the footboard, she saw it.

Poking out from one side of the bed was a human foot. Feeling her pulse racing, she forced herself to walk around the bed to that side and gasped when she realized the foot belonged to Chrissy Rockford, who was lying in a pool of her own blood. She bent down and checked for a carotid pulse, but as expected, there was none. She stared a few more minutes at Chrissy's eyes, fixed in the grotesque stare of death before she moved her gaze downward to the massive hole in her chest.

Her cop instincts kicked in, and she stood up quickly. Walking backward, she made it to the door. She took one final look before stepping into the hallway, and after covering her hand with her sweater, she closed the door behind her. This was now a crime scene and needed to be preserved for the CSI team.

Both Maddy and Tessa were waiting anxiously when she rounded the corner into the living room.

Shaking her head, she made eye contact with Lainey. "Chrissy's dead. I have to call Colt."

Chapter Seventeen

The minute Colt rushed through the door with both Flanagan and Rogers following close behind, Maddy knew she was in for the mother of all lectures. When he glimpsed his wife standing sheepishly behind her, his face tightened in anger. Maddy could almost visualize white smoke streaming from his ears.

"Where's the body?" he asked, his facial expression never changing.

Maddy pointed down the hall. "She's on the bedroom floor with a bullet to her head, probably from a 9 millimeter."

Maddy didn't think it was possible for her brother-in-law to look angrier than he already did, but when his eyes narrowed to slits, she knew she'd been wrong. She braced herself for the fallout.

"You two stay right here," he ordered. "When I come back, I'll need to have a conversation with both of you to find out why the hell you were the ones who found the body. I'm going back to the bedroom now. That should give you enough time to come up with an answer, and I can tell you, it damn well better be a good one."

Maddy made eye contact with her sister before they both nodded obediently.

Holy crap! When that boy wrinkles his face like that, grab your ass with both hands and hold on tight. I once saw him take on two guys at the same time without breaking a sweat. Tessa moved closer to her sisters in an apparent show of unity. *Don't tell him I'm here.*

So much for the unity thing.

"So what's our story, Maddy?" Lainey guided her over to the kitchen table where they both sat down to wait. "And how did you know Chrissy was shot with a nine millimeter?"

Maddy laughed. "It was a guess because it's the weapon of choice for most small time thugs. The nine millimeter is lightweight, accurate, and readily available on the street, making it one of the top five selling handguns in the country. One night while Colt and I waited for Jessie and Gracie to come out of a movie, we went for a drink. He confessed to me that at a crime scene when the M.E. or one of the CSI techs asks his opinion about what type of weapon was used, he always says a 9 millimeter. According to him, nine times out of ten, they find out he was right, and he comes off like a genius. I just used his own trick on him."

Bravo, big sis! But Lainey's right. You'd better come up with a good excuse why you were here before that man gets back. Tessa plopped down on the chair next to Lainey.

"I'm thinking we should tell him the truth—or at least some of it," Maddy said. "I'll take the lead, Lainey, and you follow, okay?"

"Got it! And Tessa's right, I have to go home with that man. If he hasn't calmed down by then, I'm in for a bad night."

They waited another fifteen minutes without speaking while Colt and the two deputies examined the crime scene. Just as the men walked out of the bedroom and headed back down the hall, the front door opened and Mark Lowell and his crew of CSI technicians strolled in, each carrying a large duffel bag.

"Who's the vic?" Mark asked Maddy before he spied Colt rounding the corner. "Hey, Sheriff, what do you have for me?"

"A young woman with a gunshot wound to her chest. No sign of the murder weapon yet, but my guess is it was a nine mil," he said, staring at Maddy when he spoke.

His message was clear. He was letting her know that it had not been lost on him that she'd remembered what he'd told her that night about guessing the caliber of the gun. For a second Maddy even saw the beginning of a smile form at the corners of his mouth before he quickly reverted back to cop face.

"When you guys give us the go-ahead, we'll do a thorough sweep of the house to see if the murder weapon turns up."

"Do we know how long she's been dead?"

Colt shook his head. "I'll send Flanagan and Rogers to canvass the neighborhood to see if they can determine the last time she was seen alive."

Aware that she was about to shoot herself right to the top of Colt's shit-list, Maddy focused on the medical examiner, not ready to address the look she knew she'd get from her brother-in-law. "We saw her yesterday around two."

"We?" Colt said, his voice accusatory.

His reaction was worse than she'd expected and his entire face was now scrunched in anger. Maddy was sure if she could see his hands, they'd be trembling.

"Maddy and I had a talk with her yesterday," Lainey said, giving her husband a glare of her own. "What do you expect us to do, Colt? Sit idly by while the evidence against Maddy piles up and she goes to prison?"

"The victim's name is Chrissy Rockford. She's the woman who caused the fight between Bernardi and the other guy at Cowboys Galore the night he was arrested," Maddy added.

Colt breathed in noisily, and Maddy was positive he was counting to ten under his breath. "I'm well aware of who she was, Maddy. We interviewed her two days ago, right after Rogers and perhaps others got her name from the bartender." His narrowed eyes staring a hole in her brain right now left no doubt he was talking about her.

"Not the bartender, Colt. It was some other lady at the bar," Rogers corrected, before falling victim to one of Colt's infamous killer stares. He slinked back behind his boss and shrugged. "I'm just sayin'."

Colt finally broke eye contact with his deputy and concentrated again on Maddy. "Did you find out anything yesterday when you spoke to her here?"

"We didn't talk to her here. We came by, but she was already gone. Her neighbor thought we were the insurance agents Chrissy had been waiting on, and she gave us a note Chrissy had left saying she'd be at another address."

"Insurance agents? Why would she think that?"

"Apparently, Chrissy had been contacted by some insurance company about a finder's fee for a piece of jewelry Bernardi had, and she was supposed to talk to the agent about it. When he didn't show up, she asked Mrs. Witherspoon, the neighbor, to watch out for him." Maddy knew she was rambling, but she kept talking anyway. As long as her mouth was moving, Colt couldn't chew them out. "The neighbor lady assumed we were from the insurance agency and sent us to another location."

"A finder's fee?" Colt asked, his face softening just a touch.

"It sounded like she had access to a necklace that had either been lost or stolen. She told her neighbor it was going to change her life," Lainey chimed in.

At the mention of the necklace, a look passed between the three cops.

"What?" Maddy asked. "Whose necklace is it?"

"You know I don't want you any more involved in this investigation than you already are, Maddy. Leave it up to us. I promise we're more capable than the Garcia girls." He paused before turning to Flanagan and Rogers. "Start knocking on doors. See if anyone noticed an unfamiliar vehicle parked on the street or a stranger that looked out of place the past few days. This had to have happened after

Maddy and Lainey left yesterday and before they arrived again today." When he was sure his deputies were out of hearing range, he glanced around the room. "Is she here?"

Maddy pointed toward Tessa who was leaning against the wall shaking her head, mouthing, *Say no, Maddy.*

"Yes."

"That's just great." He turned to his wife. "Do you have any idea how dangerous your meddling is? The killer could have been watching Chrissy's every move and just waiting for the perfect moment to take her out. I guarantee whoever this killer is, he wouldn't hesitate to kill you both on the assumption that the dead woman might have told you things he didn't want made public knowledge." He huffed. "Then the two of you could come back and haunt me like Tessa does."

"No need to get so upset, Colt. Are you forgetting that I'm a cop?"

"Yeah, you're a cop all right, but your gun is locked in the evidence locker at the station. Somehow I don't think the killer would be all that threatened by two unarmed women and a smart-ass ghost."

Lainey stepped forward and shook her finger at him. "Don't go getting sarcastic, honey," she said, drawing out the endearment in a sarcastic tone of her own. "For your information we found out something that I'd bet money you and your men don't know."

With the exception of a slight hitch in his brow, Colt's face was unreadable. "And that would be what, dear?"

"Oh no, you don't," Lainey said. "You can't holler at us like we were schoolgirls and then turn around and expect us to spill everything we learned doing exactly what you're hollering at us for. That's not how it works, darling." This time she made the endearment sound like a curse word.

Maddy bit her lower lip to keep from smiling as she watched him react to Lainey's counterattack. She knew her sister's skills as an investigative journalist were good, but she had no idea her talents were so highly polished. In a matter of seconds, she had turned Colt Winslow, a six-foot former Vineyard High School All-State halfback who commanded respect from everyone he encountered—and fear in most others—into a little boy caught talking smack to his mother.

He quickly recovered and scowled. "Not only do I expect it, Lainey, I'm prepared to throw both your asses in jail if one of you doesn't start talking in the next ten seconds."

Better spill it, ladies, before that man pops a vein in his head, Tessa said, smiling now. *I'm surprised he didn't say something snarky about me, besides the smart ass ghost thing. I'm sure he'd love to throw my dead self behind bars if for no other reason than for lying to him about Gracie way back when.*

Tessa was right. They'd pushed Colt as far as they could, counting on his tight family ties buying them some leeway, but now he was back in cop mode. It was time to come clean—or at least be a little more honest with the man. After all, he was the one running the investigation into the murder she'd been charged with.

She took a deep breath before plunging right in. "Not only did Chrissy Rockford know Gino Bernardi, but we think the two of them were running some kind of blackmail scam—probably with the married men she picked up at Cowboys Galore and who knows how many other bars around the airport."

"What makes you think that?" Colt asked, obviously interested enough to forget his anger for a few minutes.

"First of all, the note her neighbor gave us led us right to Bernardi's townhouse."

"How'd she get in?" Colt asked.

"Like I said, not only did they know each other, they were partners in some kind of illegal venture. She must've had her own key," Maddy said, wondering if she should tell him about the pictures and the notebook. She decided to hang on to those in case she needed leverage later on.

"And you two were at his place?"

Both Maddy and Lainey nodded before Maddy continued. "That's when she told us about the insurance company calling to offer a finder's fee for the necklace. We—"

"Did she say which insurance company contacted her?" he interrupted.

"No. What necklace was she talking about, Colt?" Lainey asked.

"I'd rather not say right now," he responded. "You girls already know more than I'm comfortable with. A killer who plans a murder as meticulously as this one did and manages to successfully frame an on-the-job police officer for it in the process will stop at nothing to keep his secret safe." His eyes softened. "I'm begging you to let me handle this."

"Fine," Maddy said. "You keep the information about the necklace to yourself, and we'll keep the pictures we found in Chrissy's purse our little secret."

As she watched Colt's expression quickly change back to anger, Maddy thought she had stepped over the line this time. His face now a deep shade of red, he pressed his lips together, and she heard Tessa whisper, *Uh oh* behind her back. But she was determined to find out about the necklace, and even his obvious wrath didn't stop her from standing her ground.

In her favor, she was his sister-in-law, and she knew, fair or not, he was always a little more patient with her than he was with the other guys. But more importantly, he was married to her sister, and he had to know if he ever expected to experience marital bliss again, he'd better tone down his approach.

I'll be damned! This guy can't handle any of the Garcia girls. I almost want to hug him and tell him it'll be alright.

He motioned for them to sit. "Okay. As much as it goes against every fiber in my being, every cop instinct I possess, I'll tell you what you want to know. But only after you explain about the pictures." He sat down beside Lainey on the couch. "And this better be worth it."

Maddy dug in her purse for her cell phone and pulled up the pictures she'd taken of the five guys getting oral sex from Chrissy. After handing the phone to Colt, she waited patiently while he flipped through all of them. When he came to the last one, he glanced up for a second to meet her stare before turning his attention back to the picture.

"So Foxworthy knew our victim. Maybe that's what the argument at the bar was all about."

"Yes, and we think Bernardi was taking the pictures. In every single one of them the guy looks like he's asleep," Maddy explained.

"Asleep?"

"Seriously, Colt, how many men do you think can be on the receiving end of oral sex and lie perfectly still?"

For the first time since he arrived, Colt smiled. "You've got a point, Maddy. So Chrissy picks a guy up at the bar and entices him into going to Bernardi's place where she slips him a Mickey—possibly a roofie. Then right off the bat, she and Bernardi rob the dude before getting all his personal information. My guess is the pictures start showing up in his mailbox soon after that, and the poor schlep doesn't even remember getting mind-blowing sex." He stared at the other pictures.

"Do you recognize any of the others?" Maddy asked.

Colt shook his head. "But I'm damn sure going to find out who they are. All five of them, Foxworthy included, would have had a helluva motive to kill both Bernardi and his partner in crime."

"Do you think these guys are locals?" Lainey asked.

"Probably out-of-towners on a business trip. Bernardi was smart and would have stayed away from the men who might recognize the address and come back later to make sure the pictures didn't get out," Colt said before looking up.

"We went through Chrissy's purse and didn't find these photos. After Mark and his team finish up back there, we'll tear this place apart, but from the looks of it, the killer has already done that. And if I'm right, he probably has the photos, the camera, and any computer the pictures might have been saved on."

"So we're lucky we were able to get these snapshots yesterday, right?" Maddy said, proud of herself for making copies on her phone.

He grinned. "As much as I hate to admit it, you two snoops may have just cracked this case—or at least given us another angle to pursue. Good job."

Maddy and Laney high-fived, but the elation was short-lived when Colt said, "Having said that, your sleuthing days are over, Lainey. It's getting too dangerous." He turned his attention on Maddy. "If you ever want to work as a Vineyard cop again, it would behoove you to butt out of this investigation. Am I clear?"

"Crystal," Maddy responded. "But I've always known you to be an honest man, Colt, and you gave us your word you'd tell us about the necklace after we told you what we knew."

"I do owe you that, I guess," he said. "But first I have to tell you a little story I learned from the Feebs just this morning."

Maddy's head shot up. "The FBI is involved?"

"Yes. It seems there's a guy in New York, Nicky Cavicchia, who's about to go on trial for murder and racketeering. Apparently, his bookkeeper—a guy named Joey

Agostinelli—absconded with what is rumored to be a hefty chunk of change before turning states evidence against Cavicchia. The guy I talked to said ten million was the figure being tossed around, but since these kind of businesses never really report their illegal earnings, they can only go by what a few of their snitches have reported."

Both Maddy and Lainey looked confused. "What does this have to do with the necklace?"

"I'm getting to that, Maddy, but you have to know the whole story to understand it." He glanced down at his watch. "I need to make this fast because I'm meeting one of the Feds in an hour."

"So what makes you think Bernardi was involved with the Mafia guy?" Lainey asked leaning forward with interest.

"It looks like besides the money, Agostinelli made off with a one-of-a-kind necklace that Cavicchia had specifically made for his young sexy wife out of emeralds and rare black diamonds. I've been told it was insured for two million."

"No wonder the insurance company is willing to pay a finder's fee to get it back. But I still don't understand how Bernardi got his hands on it," Maddy said, rubbing her forehead as if she had a killer migraine.

"That's what my meeting with the FBI agent is about," Colt said, glancing quickly at his watch. "It seems Gino Bernardi was missing from protective custody."

"Get out of here," Maddy said, jumping from the chair. "Why would the government protect his sorry ass?"

"Because his real name is Joey Agostinelli.

Chapter Eighteen

"Holy crap! So Bernardi, I mean Agostinelli was a mobster and turned on the head honcho?" When Colt nodded, Maddy threw her arms in the air. "Now it's all beginning to make sense," she said with a grin.

"According to the Feds, Gino Bernardi ran off with millions of Cavicchia's money and then got real chatty about his boss's business practices," Colt explained. "Given that Bernardi was executed gangster-style in his cell, I'd say your lawyer should have no problem establishing reasonable doubt, Maddy. Cavicchia certainly had motive to silence the Judas in his organization."

Maddy let out an audible sigh of relief. "Oh thank God. Now I can come back to work and get on with my life."

Colt shook his head. "I'm afraid that's not going to happen just yet. Knowing Bernardi's death was probably a mob hit and proving it are two different things. Until we find the real culprit and charges against you are dropped, or worse case scenario, it goes all the way to trial and a jury of your peers exonerates you, the suspension with pay stays in place."

Maddy huffed. She knew it wouldn't be that easy, but for a minute, she'd allowed herself to hope. "So what can we do to help?"

Colt whirled around to face her. "You must not have heard me a few minutes ago. Nothing's changed except for the fact that we now have a new lead to follow. Proving Bernardi—or should I say Agostinelli—was killed by professionals who just waltzed into the squad room and shot two prisoners while you conveniently waited in the ladies room is not going to be easy." He tsked. "Especially since they got rid of everything that ties them to coercing you by using your daughter."

"I know, Colt, but I might be able to get information out of people if they don't think I'm a cop."

"Why can't you just look at this as a paid vacation, Maddy? Spend some time with Jessie and maybe even find a hobby. Lainey was just talking about a new pottery shop opening up across from the mall. You always liked that kind of thing. Didn't you?"

"Seriously, Colt, do you honestly think I can make bowls while my life as I know it hangs in the balance?" She blew out a frustrated breath before adding, "Now get Patrick Swayze to come up behind me and caress my neck while I'm making the stupid bowl, and we're talking a whole different scenario."

His eyes reflected a glint of mischief. "You have Tessa. She doesn't have Swayze's six pack abs, but she can certainly massage your neck while you're playing in the mud."

Humor was never his longest suit, Tessa said. *But I have to say the boy is at least acknowledging that I'm here. And for the record, I do have damn good abs.*

His face turned serious again. "Whoever killed Chrissy isn't playing, Maddy. And we don't have a clue where to start looking. If the order for the hit came from New Jersey, the killer is probably long gone, but I still can't see the logic in killing Agostinelli's girlfriend. Unless they're totally unrelated. The background check on her revealed she was born and raised in Lubbock. Even went to Tech for two years before moving to Vineyard. From all indications, Joey Agostinelli only met her about two months ago, probably about the same time he landed in Vineyard to hide out from the Feds."

"She knew about the necklace," Maddy blurted. "Could it be that they tortured her before they killed her in an attempt to find it?"

Colt shook his head. "There are no signs of trauma on her body that I could see, at least not from the initial look. But the money is still out there somewhere, and that's a pretty good incentive to push the woman around to get details. The M.E. may find bruising on her abdomen, but until he tells us that's what happened, we're going to assume it didn't." He scratched his forehead. "It looks like whoever killed her marched right in and shot her in the head. I'm guessing he surprised her in the bedroom. Possibly while she was sleeping."

"So you don't think she told the killer where the money or the necklace is?" Lainey asked.

"She probably didn't know. Like I said, Agostinelli may have been running a scam with her, but I doubt he'd trust her with the knowledge about where he'd hidden ten million and the necklace."

"She said he was shopping it to foreign buyers on the black market," Maddy said, noticing that Tessa was being really quiet for some reason. She looked in that direction with a questioning look, and Tessa responded with a shrug.

"That would explain how Cavicchia got wind of where Agostinelli was hiding. He probably knew that sooner or later the guy would have to put out feelers, so he sat back and waited patiently."

"When is his trial?" Lainey asked.

"It was supposed to be several months ago, but his hotshot lawyer keeps delaying it by filing motion after motion. When Agostinelli slipped away from protective custody, the trial was put on hold. His testimony was crucial to the federal prosecutor, and now that he's dead I suspect their case will fall apart."

"What about the insurance agent who called to offer a finder's fee? Wouldn't he have a pretty good motive for wanting to get the necklace back to Cavicchia and avoid paying the two million?" Maddy asked.

"We'll be checking to see what company insured Cavicchia and find out if they made contact with Chrissy," Colt said. "That could have also been the killer's way of gaining access to her without arousing suspicion." He paused to nod to a CSI tech leaving the scene. "No matter how this turns out, I'd say the case against you is looking weaker by the minute, Maddy. Now if I can just convince you to sit back and wait while I do *my* job, I'm sure this will all be over before you know it."

"Chrissy told us the necklace is in Bern—Agostinelli's safety deposit box. She found the key in his freezer," Maddy said, slowly, staring intently at Colt's face to see his reaction.

"Why didn't you say that in the first place?" Colt turned to Rogers. "Find out where Agostinelli did his banking, and then get over to the courthouse and get a warrant from Judge Williams. We need to have a look into that box."

* * * * *

Maddy was still on a high when she headed home with her sister. Chrissy's death and finding out that Agostinelli, AKA Bernardi, was actually on the run from a Mafia godfather was the best news she'd heard all week. It meant someone else had a powerful motive for wanting the man dead.

She'd made a split second decision not to tell Colt just yet about the notebook she'd taken from Chrissy's purse. For one thing, he would have chastised her for taking it because it was illegally obtained and none of the information in it could be used in a court room. The prosecutor would call it fruit of a poisoned tree, or something like that. And next, the names in there could simply be people Bernardi thought were important and not victims like she imagined when she'd first seen them.

When she pulled up in front of her house, she spied a black pickup parked out front. *Crap!* In all the excitement of the day, she'd forgotten about Jake Matthews moving into her upstairs. She glanced down at her watch before swearing under her breath. It was almost six, and Jessie would have been home for over an hour already.

A little voice in her head screamed "bad mother" as she realized her daughter had no idea a perfect stranger was now living in their house. She hoped finding him there hadn't freaked her out.

"Looks like the tall sexy cowboy is settled in," Lainey commented before winking. "I would love to come in for another look at him, but I'm afraid Colt would have a hissy, thinking we were off snooping again. He's so worried that we'll ignore his demands to butt out of his investigation and do something stupid, he would probably send out a police car to escort me home. We aren't going to do that, are we?"

"Butt out of the investigation or do something stupid?" Maddy asked, glad to see the conversation turning away from her new tenant.

"Both. We do have to be a little more careful not to get caught, though." Lainey leaned in and high-fived her sister. "Call when you get a minute later on. I want to hear all about Jake's first night, especially if he ends up sleeping downstairs." She hitched her eyebrows several times and tapped an imaginary cigar in a comical gesture meant to intimidate the famous comedian Groucho Marx that made Maddy laugh out loud.

"Get out of here. After the way I grilled him, he'll probably stay as far away from me as he can get—which is fine by me. I just hope he didn't give Jessie a scare."

Lainey got out and walked to the driveway where her own car was parked. Maddy waved as she watched her sister pull into the street and head home. Then she drove her Honda into the garage and turned off the ignition, thinking tonight would be another take-out pizza night for sure since she hadn't had time to stop by the grocery store. The annoying little witch screaming "bad mother" made another appearance in her head.

The first thing she heard when she opened the garage door was the sound of Jessie laughing. She smiled to herself, thinking she'd worried about her for nothing. The kid was amazing and had great friends who liked to talk on the phone as much as she did. She probably hadn't even realized there was another person in the house.

Then she heard Jake's voice, although she couldn't make out what he'd said. It was immediately followed by a burst of laughter from both of them.

Oh my God! The man was in the kitchen alone with her ten-year-old daughter.

She flung the door wide open and stepped into the laundry room between the kitchen and the garage. Immediately, the smell of something cooking hit her nostrils. Nearly running now, she entered the room, and both Jessie and Jake turned with smiles still on their faces.

"Hey, Mom," Jessie began. "Jake's helping me with my homework."

Maddy glared at him. "Oh he is, is he?"

"And he's making homemade spaghetti and meatballs. Doesn't it smell awesome?"

Maddy continued to stare at Jake, who at least had the decency to wipe the smile off his face while waiting for her to say something.

When she didn't, he took a step toward her. "I hope you don't mind. I decided to make my mother's famous meatballs."

"And you thought it was okay to come down to my kitchen and be alone with my daughter?"

"Mom!" Jessie said. "He was only helping me with my homework." She turned to him and giggled. "I'll never forget the state capitals ever again, thanks to him."

Maddy forced herself not to scowl at her daughter. "Sweetie, will you let me have a minute alone with Mr. Matthews? You can finish your homework in your room."

Jessie huffed before picking up her books and notepad. "Okay, but don't take too long. I'm starving," she said, before shuffling down the hall to her bedroom.

When Maddy heard the bedroom door close behind her, she turned to Jake. "What in the hell were you thinking? That it would be okay to spend time alone with my daughter when I wasn't at home? Our agreement gives you the right to sleep upstairs, Mr. Matthews, nothing else. Nowhere does it say you're allowed to fraternize with my ten-year-old. I know you're a drunk. How do I know you're not a pervert, too?" She knew that was unfair, but all she could think about was what could have happened if he was.

His face registered the hurt at her accusations, and he held her stare for a few minutes before speaking. "First of all, let me assure you that I am abiding by your 'no drinking while in this house' rule. Second, in no way, shape, or form was my attention to your daughter sexual. I get why you're upset, though. When she got home and found me in the kitchen, I should have introduced myself and gone back upstairs. But she's such a great kid and before long she was telling me about what a hard time she was having memorizing the state capitals. I only taught her a little trick my mother showed me. I'm sorry."

Maddy took a slow breath before walking over and lifting the lid on the spaghetti sauce. It did smell divine. "We never talked about you using the kitchen," was all she could come up with.

"Again, I'm sorry. I'm tired of eating out, and I thought I'd make my mother's sauce. Figured that would keep me away from fast food for a few days at least. Frankly, I had forgotten that you'd mentioned a minor living here, so when your daughter found me in the kitchen, I was just as surprised as she was. She said you would probably bring home a pizza, and she was sick of eating that. I know I should have minded my own business, but she arrived hungry in the middle of my cooking, and I offered to share. Under the circumstances, I hoped you wouldn't mind. End of story. I had no idea you would react the way you did."

Since this was the first time she'd rented out part of her house, she wasn't up on the rules and therefore, hadn't discussed them with him. She really couldn't fault the guy for assuming the kitchen was part of the deal. And he really hadn't done anything to Jessie except make her laugh. Still, the memory of the masked gunmen standing over her daughter's bed was vivid in her mind and was enough to make even the most innocent contact with Jessie suspect in her mind.

"I was going to tell her about you tonight, but I got waylaid. I guess no harm was done. I'll get her now, and we'll head out for some supper so you can enjoy your home-cooked meal."

"There's plenty for everyone," he said. "Besides it will give me an opportunity to thank you for letting me stay upstairs. I have a pretty good lead on the investigation, and I'm hoping I'll be able to get out of your hair sooner than I thought."

All of a sudden a light bulb went off in her head. Jake said he worked for Harold's of London. Was it possible that he was the insurance agent who had made contact with Chrissy about a finder's fee? But if that were true, what did he mean by having a pretty good lead? If he was the one who made the offer to Chrissy about the stolen necklace, it was logical to believe his job would be over with now that she was dead. Then she remembered Colt mentioning that the offer of a finder's fee many have been Chrissy's killer's way of getting into her house. She had to find out what he meant.

She took a deep breath and plunged right in. No sense beating around the bush. "Are you investigating the theft of an emerald and black diamond necklace?"

His face registered surprise before he recovered. "Why would you ask that?"

"Because I talked to a woman yesterday who said she was contacted by an insurance agency about a finder's fee for that necklace. That same woman was found murdered this morning."

"Chrissy Rockford's dead?"

Bingo! She hadn't mentioned any names, and yet he knew.

"So you did contact her?" She was about to ask him if he had anything to do with her murder but decided his surprise at hearing she was dead had been genuine. She prided herself on reading people, and if he had killed her he wouldn't have been able to pull off the total surprise that took over his face when she'd told him.

He hesitated momentarily, as if deciding whether to tell her the truth. She was about to fire another question at him when he responded. "I called Chrissy the day before yesterday and made plans to meet her at her house. I've been authorized to offer her a sizable amount for the return of that necklace."

"What did she say?" Maddy asked, watching his body language to see if he would lie.

"I never got to talk to her. There was an accident on Main Street that held up traffic for thirty minutes or so. By the time I got to her house, no one was there."

Maddy gave it some thought. He must've arrived at the woman's house right after Mrs. Witherspoon had given them the note with Bernardi's address. She decided to go fishing to see if he'd tell her the truth. "Whose necklace is it?"

He shook his head. "They don't give me details like that. I'm on a need to know basis. All I know is that someone wants it back very badly and is willing to give up the insurance money to get it. I was sent here from San Antonio because my boss got information that someone from Vineyard was trying to fence it. I'd hoped to get a chance to talk to Bernardi, but we both know how that worked out. So I did the next best thing and found out his girlfriend's name. Figured he might have talked about it under the sheets one night."

"How'd you get her name?" She was beginning to get an uneasy feeling about this man, but she couldn't stop herself from digging further simply because there was a slim possibility that he had information she didn't.

"Probably from the same place you did. The good old boys at Cowboys Galore were more than willing to fill me in. All it took after that was one phone call and the mention of money, and Chrissy was all over the offer."

She eyed him suspiciously. "Is that why you rented my upstairs?"

"I have to admit it entered my mind that you might have information about the necklace," he admitted. "But it was more about me needing to stay close to Bernardi's girlfriend."

Maddy pondered that for a moment, then debated with herself whether to tell him about Bernardi's safety deposit box or the fact that the man was really Joey Agostinelli, ex bean counter for the mob. Her police instincts warned her to keep that information to herself for now. Despite her feeling that Jake was exactly who he said he was—an ex-cop now working as an insurance investigator to recover a necklace—

she wasn't about to arm him with facts about the case if it turned out her gut was wrong.

"So now what? Will you head back to San Antonio?" She couldn't help worry about how she would pay her lawyer on Friday if she had to return most of the money Jake had given her for rent.

"Probably. I'll call my boss later tonight and find out exactly what he wants me to do now." He must've noticed the look that crossed her face because he added, "A deal is a deal, Maddy. The money is yours whether I live here the full two months or not."

Just then Jessie popped her head out. "Mom, hurry up. I'm starving. Jake promised me extra meatballs."

Maddy considered insisting they would go out for fast food when she noticed Jake setting the table with three plates. Her instincts continued to scream for her to stay away from this man, but when she saw her daughter bound out of her bedroom and plop down at the table, she gave in. What would it hurt if they ate one meal with their new tenant?

She still didn't fully trust the guy, but the smell of the sauce plus her daughter's excitement was too tempting to pass up. Jessie was right. They had been eating a lot of pizza lately, and a home-cooked meal sounded delightful. After they'd found Chrissy's body there hadn't been time for her and Lainey to grab lunch. All she'd had to eat all day was the breakfast sandwich and the pastry. Her stomach chose that particular moment to growl as if to let her know it was well aware of that fact.

She pursed her lips to keep from smiling then sat down opposite her daughter. Nothing more was said as Jake dished up the spaghetti then turned his back on them to open the oven and pull out a tray of garlic Texas toast. For the first time she noticed how narrow his waist looked in his tight jeans, deciding his entire backside didn't look too shabby, either. And at least for now, the little voice in her head critiquing her mothering skills was gone.

When he finally sat down with his own plate, she took her first bite and nearly moaned. It was that good. As she swirled the pasta around her fork, she decided, if necessary, she could always throw his cute little butt out of her house tomorrow.

Chapter Nineteen

Maddy woke up the next day in a good mood. Maybe it was the fact that there was now evidence to prove she wasn't the only one who could have killed Agostinelli. Sounded weird calling him that. Even weirder thinking of him as an accountant with the balls to not only run off with millions of the mob boss's money, but also to snag a prize necklace belonging to the man's wife on his way out.

But if she was being honest, she'd have to admit there was another reason for her good spirits. Last night after devouring Jake's fantastic spaghetti dinner, they'd all sat around and talked for over an hour while he did the dishes. Said it was his treat and wouldn't even let either her or Jessie get up from the table to help.

It had warmed Maddy's heart to see her daughter having so much fun with him. Jess was born three months before her father was killed in Afghanistan, and since that time, her Uncle Colt had been the only true male figure in her life.

When Maddy was finally alone with her daughter in the bedroom, she had been surprised to hear her babble on and on about Jake. If it hadn't been a school night she would've probably given in to her pleas to stay up for one more hour.

When Maddy had returned to the kitchen, she'd thanked Jake again for the dinner. A niggling twinge of guilt for calling him a drunk earlier played in her mind, and she tried to find the right way to address it.

Truth be told, he'd been on his best behavior all night, and for that she was grateful. She'd almost hated to think of him leaving so soon even though he'd assured her she could keep the money he'd paid for the rent and deposit. If circumstances were different, she wouldn't even entertain the idea of keeping his money, but she was desperate.

Despite all the new information pointing to reasonable doubt in her case, her trial would still go on. And Anthony Pirelli was stopping by in an hour for his retainer, among other things. Discount or not, the man didn't come cheap.

She promised herself she'd send Jake a refund check as soon as her bottom line looked a little better. She and Jess had already been living on frozen dinners and five-dollar pizzas for the past month. A few more weeks of that wouldn't hurt anything, except Maddy's waistline.

That's why the spaghetti dinner the night before had tasted so good.

She found herself humming while she fixed Jessie's breakfast and brewed herself a cup of coffee. Just as her daughter was finishing her cereal, Jake walked in, looking like he'd just stepped out of the shower. Immediately Jessie's face lit up.

He eyed the box of Frosted Flakes in front of the ten-year old. "Got any more of that?"

Maddy was surprised he hadn't commented on her daughter's unhealthy breakfast. She nodded. "Want a cup of coffee and a banana to go with it?"

He bent down and wiped a dab of milk from Jessie's chin before sitting down opposite her. "Absolutely. How did you know Frosted Flakes were my favorite?"

"They're mine, too," Jessie said, her smile so wide Maddy thought her lips would split. What was it about this man that had her daughter mesmerized?

For the next ten minutes while they ate, Jake quizzed the child on the state capitals, and to Maddy's surprise, Jessie didn't miss a single one. Apparently his little trick had worked.

After she saw Jessie to the school bus and came back into the house, Maddy snuck a quick glance at the clock in the living room. She had thirty-five minutes before Tony Pirelli and his legal team were scheduled to arrive for a full day of strategizing. She couldn't wait to tell him about the latest developments in the case.

"I spoke to my boss last night," Jake said as soon as she walked into the kitchen. "He wants me to stay in Vineyard a few more days to see if I can work with the cops on getting the necklace back to the rightful owner. Will that be a problem?"

"You've paid me for two months. Why would two days be a problem?"

He held her stare. "I think last night turned out okay, but I get the feeling you'll be glad to get me out of your hair."

She licked her dry lips. "About last night, I'm sorry. I overreacted. All I could picture when I saw you with Jessie was the masked man who—"

"What masked man?" he interrupted.

She drew in a deep breath and expelled it slowly. The paper hadn't reported her story about the cell phone in the drawer the night Agostinelli was killed, and she was unsure if she wanted to get into this with him. But something in his eyes, now so full of concern, made her trust him, and she told him the whole story.

"Jesus!" he exclaimed. "No wonder you went ballistic last night." He lowered his voice as if Jessie was still close by and might hear. "And you're positive your daughter has no idea about all this?"

"Neither she nor her grandmother knew anything about it until it was over. I was the one who scared them to death when I called and freaked out."

"I would've done the same thing." He got up from the table. "So do the police think Bernardi's murder was a professional hit?"

"Agostinelli," she corrected before she caught herself. She hadn't meant to say that. The dead man's mob connection had not been made pubic knowledge yet.

"That explains a lot," he said, after a moment. When she questioned him with her eyes, he responded, "I keep up with the news, especially when it's about the cops catching a bad guy. I've heard his name mentioned along with a gangster from New Jersey who's getting ready to go on trial for murder."

"It seems our dead guy was in protective custody until a few months ago," Maddy confirmed.

"So, I'm guessing the client looking for the return of the necklace is said gangster from New Jersey?"

She nodded. What did it matter if he knew? He would be leaving for San Antonio in a few days anyway. She felt his intense stare, and she looked up. "I'm sorry I called you a drunk last night."

A slow grin crossed his face. "You were right. I am a drunk, but I've kept my promise not to indulge myself while I'm in your house. Now that I've met your daughter, you can be certain I'll keep that promise."

"I read all the reviews on you, and from all indications you were a decorated homicide detective."

His eyebrows hitched as he met her stare. "Still checking up on me, I see."

"Seriously, after what I just told you about the armed stranger standing over my daughter while she slept, do you blame me?"

"No," he admitted. "You would have been remiss not to have fully vetted me." He stared up at her. "What else did you find out?"

"Not much other than what you've already told me about your partner being killed. Things seemed to fall apart for you after that."

His short laugh held no humor. "You could say that."

"I can't even imagine how I would feel if my partner was killed. What happened at the drug bust?" She knew she was skirting dangerously close to none–of–your–business territory, but she couldn't stop now.

This time it was his turn to breathe deeply and slowly expel it. "My partner wasn't just killed. It was my screw up that cost him his life."

She watched as he lowered his head and realized that this was still very painful for him to talk about. "Is that when you started drinking heavily?"

"Alcohol was the only thing that kept me sane."

She took a step toward him and patted his shoulder. "We all have our demons, Jake. Sooner or later you're going to have to forgive yourself."

He moved away from her touch as if it was a hot iron. "Easier said than done." He tried to smile. "I'll just go upstairs and let you get on with your day."

"Oh, I forgot to tell you. My lawyer's bringing his legal team here in about an hour. We'll be working on my case for the rest of the morning."

"Then I'll definitely stay upstairs. I have a lot of paperwork that will keep me busy. Unless you prefer I take my work down to Starbucks while they're here."

"Your choice, although relaxing at Starbucks would probably be much nicer than being stuck in the room the rest of the morning."

He laughed. "You've convinced me. I'll just grab my things from upstairs and head that way." He turned and started up the steps. Halfway up, he stopped and faced her. "I can't believe anybody who knows you could think you're capable of killing a man in cold blood." Then he walked the rest of the way to his room.

When she heard his door close, she felt an overwhelming empathy for the guy. Knowing you were the reason someone was dead was bad enough, but if that someone had been a friend, it had to be much more painful. She vowed to cut him some slack his last few days as her tenant.

Once the house was empty, Maddy put on another pot of coffee and waited for her lawyer. He called to say he was bringing doughnuts, but there was no way she could eat anything. She didn't know why her stomach was doing flip-flops right now. Everything seemed to be going her way, for a change. She had the ten thousand dollar check ready for Pirelli and new information that should make his job easier. So why was she suddenly feeling so apprehensive?

She jumped when the doorbell rang.

Better get that, sis. High dollar lawyers don't like to be kept waiting.

She glanced over her shoulder to see Tessa padding behind her to the door. "So you finally decided to show up."

What do you mean finally? I was with you and Lainey all day yesterday. I pop in when you need me.

"And why would I need you today? I'm just going to go over the facts of my case with my lawyer."

Tessa grinned. ***Okay, you got me. This appearance is strictly sexual in nature. I wanted another look at that gorgeous hunk who's gonna save your ass.***

Maddy eyed her suspiciously. "So you can control when you show up."

No, but for some reason the powers that be must have thought you needed me today. The eye candy on the other side of the door is just gravy. Tessa hitched an eyebrow. *Better let him in. Time is money with these guys.*

Maddy opened the door, surprised to see that Pirelli had only brought two other people with him, both of whom looked young enough to be college students. When he said he was bringing his team, she imagined it would consist of six or seven seasoned lawyers all working together to find the evidence that would prove her innocence.

As if Tessa read her mind, she said, *Guess ten grand doesn't buy you much nowadays.*

Tony Pirelli pushed the door open and walked in. "Let's set up in the dining room," he instructed his assistants who were each carrying a box of files. They followed him to the dining room table and sat down.

"Maddy, this is John Rocha and Betsy Morgan. Both are fourth-year associates and very good at what they do."

After shaking hands with them, Maddy went to the kitchen to prepare a tray with coffee and the fixings. After placing it on the table, she opened the hutch drawer and pulled out the check. When she handed it to Pirelli, he looked surprised, as if he hadn't really believed she could get that much money together in so short a time.

But he quickly recovered and smiled. "Thank you. I'll get the ball rolling on hiring a few private investigators to dig for information in places we can't."

When everyone had a steaming cup of coffee in front of them, they made small talk while they feasted on the doughnuts. Maddy grabbed her own cup of coffee and sat down opposite her lawyer, ready to scream, "Eat the bloody food and let's get on with it."

She took a quick breath to try to settle her nerves. Finally, Pirelli removed several file folders from the box in front of him and motioned for the others to do the same.

"We've been concentrating on who else wanted Bernardi dead. We're all in agreement that a reasonable doubt verdict will be easier to pull off than trying to explain away the evidence against you." He opened the folder and lifted out a sheet of paper.

Before he could explain what it was, Maddy interrupted.

"Agostinelli's girlfriend was murdered yesterday, and Colt—Sheriff Winslow—has proof that she and the dead guy were working some kind of scam."

"Agostinelli?"

She was getting ahead of herself. She poured another cup of coffee and leaned back in her chair. Then she told him everything she knew about the dead man's mob connections, as well as the information she had about the alleged scam he and Chrissy had been running on married men. She fully expected him to react positively to the news and was puzzled to see his face scrunched in deep thought instead.

Finally he spoke. "So the sheriff thinks this may have been a mob hit?"

She nodded. "There's a man in New Jersey about to go on trial for murder. The Feds were counting on Agostinelli's testimony to put him away. I'd say that's a pretty powerful motive for wanting to silence the guy, wouldn't you?"

For the first time since she'd started telling the story, Pirelli smiled. "Without a doubt. This just may be your 'get out of jail free' card." He turned to his assistants. "Check with the New Jersey Attorney General's office and find out what's going on." He twisted back to face Maddy. "Do we know the name of this New Jersey man?"

"Cavicchia."

After scribbling the name on the front of the folder, Pirelli barked out several more orders before he settled his attention again on Maddy. "And you say Bernardi, I mean Agostinelli and his girlfriend were running a scam on married men? What kind of evidence do the cops have?"

"Pictures of the woman giving oral sex to several unconscious men."

"But no proof of blackmail or any victims willing to come forward?"

Maddy shook her head. "The Vineyard police are trying to track down the men in the pictures as we speak."

He blew out a frustrated breath. "So right now all they have is a bunch of pictures of naked people. One could argue that the girlfriend simply liked seeing herself getting guys off. Blackmail will be hard to prove without victims or money transfers."

Darn it! She hadn't thought of that. Maybe she needed to go on a little fishing expedition down at the station and see if she could find out any information about the men in the pictures. That would definitely mean sneaking around Colt to do it, because if he found out she was snooping after his explicit orders not to even think about it, he'd made it perfectly clear he'd fire her.

She decided it was time to play the Danny Landers card. Have Kate dress up in a silky blouse with several opened buttons in the front and work her magic on the youngest cop on the force who had always had a thing for her youngest sister.

Then she remembered she hadn't told Pirelli about the necklace. "I almost forgot. Apparently, Agostinelli made off with a very expensive necklace belonging to Cavicchia's wife. The police were going to get a warrant today and search his safety deposit box at the bank."

At the mention of the necklace, Pirelli's head shot up from the file he'd been reading. "Do you know if they found it there?"

She shook her head. "They don't keep me in the loop these days," she said with more sarcasm than she intended.

Pirelli glanced at his watch then gathered the folders that were spread across the table and put them back into the box. "Thanks to you I've got more than enough to keep these two busy for a few days. On my way out of Vineyard, I'll stop by the police station and have a chat with Sheriff Winslow to see what information he's willing to give me."

"That's a good idea. I'll use my sources to find out anything I can, too."

He nodded toward the door as a signal to his associates to head that way. "I'll give you a call on Monday to update you on our progress. In the meantime, sit tight. These things take a lot of time and patience if they're done right. We don't want to rush it and miss something vital."

Maddy followed them to the door and watched the assistants get into a compact car parked next to the curb. Pirelli walked to his red Cadillac Escalade in the driveway.

You can tell the peons from the non-peons by their toys. Tessa said, moving in front of Maddy to get a better look at Pirelli's backside. *Umm umm umm! As fantastic as his backside looks in that silk suit that must have cost a small fortune, I'm wondering if the guy is as good as he says he is. Why'd he have to hear the story about Agostinelli from you?*

"This only happened yesterday, Tessa," Maddy said.

Tessa huffed. *Seems like he and his 'very good at what they do' flunkies should have been all over that on their own. The guy might be smokin' hot in the looks department, but I'm beginning to question his ability to save your skin.*

"Cut him some slack. After all, he does have a ninety percent success rate."

She smirked. *Let's hope you're not gonna become part of that lower ten percent statistic.*

* * * * *

Anthony Pirelli couldn't get out of his client's house fast enough. When she'd dropped the bomb about the necklace, he knew he'd hit pay dirt. That information would score major points for him in New Jersey. He hoped she hadn't noticed his initial surprise when she'd told him that Bernardi was actually Agostinelli. His boss wouldn't be real happy when he heard that. They hadn't counted on the hayseed cops figuring that out so soon.

He reached for his cell phone, glad he'd insisted the two associates bring their own vehicle, and he dialed the number labeled *NJ*. When he heard the voice on the other end, he said, "They know about Agostinelli, and they think they've found your necklace."

Chapter Twenty

You can't be serious, Kate. That old blouse will never make Danny Landers look up from his boring police reports. Tessa strolled over to Kate's closet to check out a few other possibilities. Shaking her head, she motioned to Maddy to come over and help her choose something else. *We need to do some serious improvising here, girl. From the looks of these clothes, it looks like our Kate has been shopping at the second hand stores.*

Maddy grabbed Deena's arm and propelled her toward the other side of the room where Tessa waited by the closet. "Tessa thinks we need to find Kate something a little sexier." She bit back a smile. "She's not really impressed with your wardrobe, Katie. Wants to know if you've been bargain hunting at Goodwill again?"

Kate huffed. "Tell that smart aleck I'm not as conniving as she was, nor did I marry a jerk-off just for his money." She narrowed her eyes "Where is she, anyway?" After Maddy pointed to the empty spot beside her, Kate took several steps forward, her finger pointed. "And, sister dearest, need I remind you that I work eighteen hours a day in scrubs? My social life consists of catching up on my sleep and watching taped reality TV on my days off. There's really no reason for fancy clothes that I can't afford on my resident's salary anyway."

Touché, little sis. I should have left you more money in my will. Tessa went through the closet piece by piece, finally settling on a silky red and aqua blouse. *Hand her this one, Maddy.*

Maddy reached around her dead sister and pulled out the shirt. "Got any black skinny jeans to go with this?" She held it up for Kate to see.

"Matter of fact, I do," Kate said, grabbing the shirt and throwing it on the bed before rummaging through the bottom drawer of the dresser for her jeans. When she found the pair she wanted, she yanked the blouse she was wearing over her head.

My God! The girl is twenty-seven years old and surprisingly, has a nice rack. You'd think she'd at least have one or two Victoria's Secret bras lying around somewhere. Doesn't she dress provocatively for that neurosurgeon she's been seeing? The guy looks at gray matter all day long for a living. Shouldn't he be treated to a little skin at night?

Maddy threw her arm out just as Kate prepared to slip the new blouse over her head. "Do you have a push-up bra, kiddo? Surely, you get dolled up for your doctor friend once in a while." She winked at Tessa.

Kate scrunched her nose. "I dumped him about a week ago. Thought I'd told you."

Oh boy, her relationships last about as long as mine did. Looks like she's getting more and more like me every day.

Deena, who was the most empathetic of the Garcia sisters, reached out and hugged Kate. "I'm sorry, dear. Are you okay?"

Kate growled. "Glad to be rid of him, actually. He acted like I should bend over and kiss his ring because he was a brain surgeon."

Our girl broke up with the good doctor over religious differences. Tessa chuckled. *He believed he was God, and she didn't.*

Maddy smiled before turning back to Kate. "Sounds like you're better off. It wouldn't be such a hardship to have a little fun with Danny Landers, would it? God knows you need it after looking at the female anatomy all day long. Plus, he's been eyeing you up ever since junior high."

"I know," she said. "I just can't picture him as a serious boyfriend. He's so immature about everything." She pursed her lips. "He does make me laugh, though."

"That's not a bad thing. Lainey swears if Colt didn't bring a smile to her face every now and then, he'd be out the door. Says he can be such a pain in the butt sometimes." Maddy shrugged. "Her words, not mine."

"They can all be jerks in the right moment," Deena chimed in before she lowered her eyes, a response not lost on either sister.

Both Maddy and Kate were at her side in a flash. "Deena, is everything all right with you and Mike?" Kate asked.

Deena shook her head and swiped at the lone tear escaping down her cheek. "I'm pretty sure he's cheating on me again."

"Oh, honey, I'm so sorry," Maddy said. "Have you talked to him about it?"

This time she nodded. "I confronted him last week after I did the laundry and smelled perfume on his shirt. Although he denied it, I'm positive he's up to his old tricks again."

"Maybe it was something innocent," Maddy said, rubbing her younger sister's back and hoping her voice didn't betray her. Mike Hernandez was and probably always would be a womanizing snake, but she knew saying that out loud would only make Deena feel like she had to defend him.

"After he fell asleep, I went through his wallet and found a receipt from a swanky hotel in downtown Dallas." Deena sniffed back more tears. "The cheapskate wouldn't even let me buy a new bedspread."

No words were necessary as Deena allowed her sisters to comfort her. Finally she looked up and attempted a smile. "I think it's time to cut my losses and run. I'm sick of all the lying and cheating. Truth be told, I've suspected for a long time that all those late business meetings were bogus. Guess I just didn't care enough to check it out." A glint of mischief replaced the tears. "And it's not like he was a fireball in bed, anyway."

"You know whatever you decide, we'll be right beside you holding your hand, right?" Maddy said. "And now that I've gotten a reputation as a cold-blooded killer, maybe I can even scare him a little."

Deena laughed out loud. "That shouldn't be funny, but it is." She kissed both her sisters on the cheek. "Come on. We're not here today to talk about my marital problems. We've got to get Kate all sexed up so she can squeeze Danny for the information." Turning to Kate, she said, "Here. Let me help with this so you don't mess up your hair too much."

"Wait." Kate walked to the dresser and pulled out a black lace bra. "Just so you know, Maddy, I've turned a head or two with this in the past." Quickly she peeled off the old bra and put on the push-up one.

Big difference! That boy won't be able to keep his eyes off her boobs, Tessa said.

"Danny will be all over you like a big red rash," Deena said, causing another round of laughter as she used the phrase made famous by their stepdad. "Maybe it'll turn into something more than just a fishing expedition."

Kate sighed. "You are such a romantic, Deena. I have no time for dating, although it would be nice to be able to spend some of my off-duty time with someone who makes me laugh."

Now you're really thinking like me, Tessa said. ***Keep a stud fully charged somewhere in an out-of-the-way place where you can get to him when you need him.*** She winked. ***Kinda like a Dustbuster.***

When Maddy repeated what Tessa had said, both Kate and Deena giggled. It was nice to see Deena with her mind off her dirtbag of a husband, at least for the time being. Maddy promised herself she'd sit down with her sister over coffee in the next day or so and let her talk it out.

Secretly, she admitted to herself that she wouldn't shed any tears if Deena decided to dump the loser and get on with her life. But she also knew that no matter the reason, divorce was hard on both parties, and her sister would need her best friend there for support.

But all that would have to wait. Right now they were on a mission to find out the names of the men in those pictures with Chrissy. In order to do that, they'd have to make Kate irresistible enough to get Danny Landers to defy his boss's explicit orders and talk.

She took a step toward her younger sister and unbuttoned the top two buttons on the blouse, allowing a little of the cleavage to peek out. It was just enough to entice a horny deputy who had always had a thing for her baby sister into letting her have a look at a couple of reports.

"I'm ready," Kate said with a newfound confidence. "Take me to my prey."

"That's my girl," Maddy said. "Now go put on some makeup. You have a big job ahead of you."

* * * * *

As soon as Maddy opened the door and walked into the police station with Kate and Deena following close behind, her stomach began doing gymnastics. She'd known Colt Winslow all her life and hated that she was going behind his back. But her biggest concern was that because he did know her so well, he'd see right through her facade.

They'd purposely left Lainey out of the plan to allow her some degree of deniability. After all, she was the one who would have to face Colt every night and listen to his reprimand. And there definitely would be hell to pay if he found out. No, the less he believed his wife knew, the better.

On the drive over, they'd concentrated on getting their stories straight so as not to arouse suspicion. Maddy knew all her coworkers would be glad to see her without thinking she might have an ulterior motive. Not so with her brother-in-law. It was now or never for them to find out if she or her sisters could win an Academy Award with their performances.

As expected, everyone rushed over and gave her a hug as soon as she walked in. She had to bite her lower lip to keep from smiling at Danny Lander's reaction when he spotted Kate. She almost felt sorry for him.

"Hi, Danny," Kate said with a phony shy smile. "You're looking good."

The poor boy couldn't keep his eyes off her, and at one point Maddy thought he actually might have drooled. Over the past year, the only time he'd seen Kate was when she was in scrubs or an oversized T-shirt. Checking out her sexy skinny jeans and the low-cut blouse she was wearing plus the fact that she had on makeup, the man looked like he was about to swoon.

"What are you doing here, Maddy?" Colt asked, appearing out of nowhere with a stern look on his face.

"Oh hi, Colt. The station is the first stop on a much-needed Garcia girls' day out. We're treating Kate to lunch at Ruby's since it's her first real day off in weeks." She smiled as sweetly as she could, glad he couldn't see her hands trembling. "Then we're going to hit the spas—hair, nails, and toes. Maybe even that new body massage place off Main Street." She paused as she watched his face, convinced he wasn't buying her story. "No guys allowed," she added for emphasis, worried it might be overkill.

"Why isn't Lainey going with you?"

Crap! They hadn't thought that far ahead to come up with an excuse. Of course he'd wonder why his wife wasn't joining her sisters on their adventure.

"She's meeting us at Ruby's," Deena said, just moments before Maddy was about to fess up to the real reason they were at the station. "She had a few errands to run while we stopped by here."

Well, I'll be! I don't think I've ever heard Deena tell a lie in her entire life.

Maddy glanced over her shoulders and made eye contact with Tessa.

Solidarity! Tessa said. ***Looks like the cat's got Danny Lander's tongue.*** She pointed to where the young cop stood staring at Kate, almost mesmerized. ***Probably a few more parts of his anatomy are stiff, too.***

"So why did you stop here first?" Colt asked. "I made it perfectly clear about you snooping around."

Maddy huffed. "Who says I'm snooping around? The station was on our way to Ruby's, and we decided to stop by for a few minutes. That's all."

His eyes burned into her. "Why?"

Maddy blew out a slow breath. Out of the corner of her eye, she could see that Kate had managed to get Danny cornered by his desk and was chatting him up. She had to give her sister a little time to break through his police barriers or all the acting in the world wouldn't get them what they needed.

"We came by to pick up Deena's lunch container." When he looked confused, she added, "She brought me a turkey sandwich and her famous Pumpkin Pie Crunch Thursday night when—" She was interrupted when Jeannie Alexander walked over.

"Colt, the mayor's on the phone and needs to talk to you ASAP."

Maddy smiled at the girl who had replaced her when she'd gone off to the police academy. "Hey, Jeannie, how's your baby girl?"

"She's doing much better, Maddy. The doctor said it was only a virus. We miss you a lot," she said before turning her attention back to Colt. "The mayor said it was really important."

Colt hesitated briefly as it trying to decide if keeping the mayor waiting was worth it to make sure Maddy didn't ask questions about her case. Apparently, he decided the former was not in the best interest of his job security.

"Tell the mayor I'll be there in a minute," he said to Jeannie, before nailing Maddy with his eyes once again. "Make it quick. Kate is causing quite a distraction to my young officers." He did a one-eighty and headed back toward his office.

Good call on the lunchbox, Maddy. Tessa said, following her and Deena to the other room.

Maddy opened the door to the break room and took her time walking to the refrigerator. She was sure the sandwich would be long gone, but she prepared herself for the sight in case it wasn't. Chances of that happening were slim to nil, though, as no food item was ever safe with the guys around. Unless, of course, it was celery sticks or a protein shake.

Not seeing the container, Maddy checked the freezer. Not there, either. Slowly, she opened every cabinet, hoping to give her younger sister more time to work her thing with Landers. The container was nowhere to be found, which was strange. Food anywhere in the break room was considered fair game, but usually no one pilfered the containers, for no other reason than they didn't want to clean them.

"Find what you're looking for?"

Maddy nearly shrieked at the sound of Colt's voice. She shook her head.

"Mike will have a fit if we don't find it," Deena said. "It's one of those new insulated carriers that he bought to take cold food to his office, and he's been asking about it." She turned to Maddy. "Check again. He'll kill me if I don't come home with it."

That makes twice my sister has lied. Tessa tsked. *What's this world coming to?*

Maddy's elation at having a reason to spend a little extra time searching was short lived as Colt sat down in the chair by the door.

"I'll just wait here until you're through," he said with a grin.

The man definitely knew they were up to something.

After another check of every cabinet still didn't turn up the missing lunch pail, Maddy shrugged. "Okay, then. Guess we'll have to stop by Target on the way home and pick up another one for Mike." She grabbed Deena's elbow. "Come on. Let's blow this honky-tonk and get some of Ruby's famous chicken fried steak." She smiled at Colt as she passed. "Too bad you're a guy, or we'd invite you to go with us."

His raised eyebrows indicated he hadn't bought the finding-Mike's-lunch-box story. He was still deep in thought, probably trying to figure out the real reason for their trip. After waiting until they were completely out of the break room, he followed behind them and shut the door.

"Kate, we don't get to see enough of you around here," he said loud enough to be heard across the room where his sister-in-law was now sitting on the edge of Danny's desk, laughing at something the officer had said. "Of course, no one would get much work done if you came by more often," he said, specifically for his young deputy's benefit.

Danny jumped up as if he'd been caught slowly stripping Kate's clothes off with his hands instead of his eyes. "I was just telling her how we run an investigation, Colt."

"I hope you didn't bore her with too many details." Colt tried without success to make his remark sound flippant, but failing miserably. The man was obviously more than a little worried.

He grabbed Maddy's arm and guided her to the door. "Tell my wife I'll be home late tonight." He waited for all three sisters to exit.

Once they were far enough away not to be overheard, Deena said, "Sheesh! He couldn't get us out of there fast enough. Do you think he was onto us?"

Maddy nodded. "Oh hell yeah! He was definitely not buying the lunch pail story."

"That was a good one, by the way," Deena said. "I had totally forgotten about it."

"Thought you said Mike had just gotten it and insisted on using it to bring the leftovers to me at work Thanksgiving night."

"That's true, but he hasn't even mentioned it since. Guess he wasn't that impressed with it."

They piled into Maddy's car without bringing up the subject of the reason for their trip to the station in the first place. Maddy was sure Kate hadn't had enough time to work on Danny, especially with Colt's suspicions on high alert and with him watching Maddy like a store detective would a suspected shoplifter.

"Doesn't anyone want to know about me and Danny?" Kate asked from the back seat.

"I'm sorry we couldn't stall any longer, honey, but Colt wasn't about to let us out of his sight," Deena said.

"I had forgotten how cute Danny really is," Kate said. "I think I'd be okay with him as my Dustbuster," she said with a laugh. "Where is Tessa, anyway?"

Maddy glanced in the rearview mirror and waved at the ghost. "Right beside you."

Kate turned in that direction. "You would have been so proud to see me in action, sis. I must've learned something from you after all these years."

Wish I could have stayed around long enough to teach you the really good stuff. Tessa sighed. *I didn't even get to make my bucket list.*

Maddy ignored her middle sister and concentrated on the younger one. "Did you find out anything useful with all that flirting?"

Kate giggled. "I told him I was fascinated by the TV shows that were able to take a face in the crowd and run a facial recognition program on the computer to identify that person."

Maddy's head jerked up. "And?"

"He laughed. Said it wasn't that easy."

"Darn it!" Deena said. "So we got nothing."

"Hold your horses, girls. Didn't you hear me say Tessa would have been proud of me?"

Maddy took a left turn into the parking lot at Ruby's diner and spotted an open space right up front. After she pulled in and turned off the engine, she said, "Please say he told you the names of the men in the pictures."

Kate shook her head. "He's a cop. He wouldn't do that."

Maddy's hope plummeted, and she opened the car door. "Oh well, it would have been a good idea if it had worked. At least we've got Ruby's home cooking to soften our disappointment."

"Who said we were disappointed?"

Maddy pulled the door shut and twisted to face her sister in the backseat. "You implied he didn't give you any names."

Kate licked her lips, smug look on her face. "He didn't, but he pulled out a folder labeled CHRISSY RUTHERFORD'S PHOTOS. Said although they didn't have the sophisticated equipment that the TV guys did, they were able to run a facial recognition with a new computer program being tested nationwide. Unfortunately, the only people in the data bank right now are ones with prior felony convictions."

"Oh," Deena moaned. "You had my hopes up for a second."

Kate frowned. "Why do you doubt me so, Deena? I told you. I learned from the Master." She high fived the air as if she actually could see Tessa. "Once I saw the folder, I pretended like I was dying of thirst and asked where I could get a cold drink. Of course he offered to get one for me."

Maddy couldn't stop herself from feeling the hope ascending back to the top of her emotions. "You peeked into that folder while he was gone?"

"I did. I made sure my back was facing everyone so they couldn't see me, and I did a quick look inside."

Maddy gasped. "Please tell me one of Chrissy victims was a felon and you saw his name."

Kate grinned. "Better than that, Maddy. Two of the men in those pictures were convicted felons, but I knew I'd never remember the names. You know how bad I am at memorizing things."

"So we're back to square one," Deena said, blowing out a frustrated breath.

"Not exactly." Kate shoved her phone toward the front seat. "You gotta love these gadgets. I may not be able to remember names, but when you have them on your smart phone, along with pictures, who cares?"

Chapter Twenty-One

Maddy stared at the first picture on Kate's phone. It was the DMV photo of a Hispanic man who appeared to be in his late thirties. His name was Francis Montero, and according to his driver's license, he lived in East Dallas near Fair Park.

She flipped to the next photo. It was another driver's license of a second Hispanic man, Joseph Gutierrez. This one lived in Abilene, a town about 150 miles west of Fort Worth. Gutierrez appeared younger, possibly in his late twenties. Neither man looked like the type who'd need help finding female companionship. But being in an airport bar away from the family and having a hot blonde offering things that might not be available at home could prove to be too tempting for some men. Add a few beers to the mix, and even the most conservative of travelers might give in to fifteen minutes of no-questions-asked sex.

"Let me have a look, Maddy," Deena said, snatching the phone from her sister's hand. After she studied both pictures, she looked up and shrugged. "Frankly, neither one looks like a killer."

"Nor did Ted Bundy," Kate remarked from the backseat.

She's got a point, Tessa said. ***They think you're a killer, Maddy, and you sure don't look the part.***

Maddy acknowledged Tessa's remark with a nod before focusing back on Kate. "Did you get a chance to see what these two did to earn felony convictions?" She reached for the phone from Deena's outstretched hand and studied the pictures once again.

Kate shook her head. "I barely had time to snap these before I heard Colt's voice behind me. I almost peed my pants, sure he'd caught me in the act." She blew out a relieved breath. "I'm not cut out for this kind of stuff. I'll take a breach delivery over this any day."

"I could ask Rogers for the info, but he's already in enough trouble with Colt for helping me." Maddy handed the phone back to Kate. "Text these to me, please. I think I'll start with the East Dallas guy before driving all the way to Abilene on a wild goose chase."

"If you check on him tomorrow, I can go with you," Kate offered. "I don't have to be back at the hospital until after four."

"I'd love the company. We can do an early lunch beforehand and then go see Mr..." Maddy picked up her phone when she heard the ding signaling the arrival of the text from Kate's cell. "Mr. Francis Montero. We'll see what he has to say about how he handled finding out there were photographs of him and Chrissy. I'll call him first thing tomorrow morning and set up a meeting."

"What if he did kill both Chrissy and Agostinelli? Aren't you just a little worried that he might take exception to our asking questions? You don't even have a gun anymore, Maddy," Kate said.

"By tomorrow I will have come up with a good reason why we're there without seeming like we're threatening him. But just in case, I'll throw Robbie's old forty-five into my purse."

"I can't make it," Deena said with a sigh. "Tomorrow is field trip day at the nursing home. We're taking the residents to the Dallas Arboretum to see the winter flowers, and I'm the only one who can drive the van. Shoot!"

"It will probably be a bust, anyway," Kate said. "This dude doesn't look like he has the balls to *plan* a double murder, much less carry it out."

"Now would be a good time to remind you of your own words, Kate. Actually two words—Ted Bundy." Maddy clicked off her phone and shoved it into her purse. "Come on. Lainey's probably been here for a while, and you know how she gets when she has to wait."

* * * * *

The next morning came way too soon for Maddy after she and her sisters had spent a perfect day getting pampered. They should have an excuse to have a pamper day more often, preferably not to save anyone from jail next time.

And they now had two new leads to work on.

She took another sip of her coffee and leaned back in the chair, smiling as she watched Jake clear away the breakfast dishes. She could get used to being waited on. Too bad all good things eventually come to an end.

"You're wrapping up your case and heading back to San Antonio today?" she asked, suddenly feeling a little sad. She was just getting to know Jake and would have liked a few more days with him before sending him on his merry way. She hadn't realized how much she'd missed being in the company of a man who made her laugh.

Maybe she should take Tessa's advice and get a Dustbuster of her own.

"Actually it's tomorrow," he replied, as he cleared the breakfast table. "I'm meeting with Sheriff Winslow today to finalize the details of the necklace. Then I'll head out first thing the following morning."

"So they did find the necklace in the safety deposit box yesterday?"

Jake nodded. "The money wasn't there, though. Upwards of ten million was reported stolen last year and may never be recovered."

"What a shame. I could definitely use a little of that myself."

He met her eyes and held them. "About the money. I meant what I said about you keeping it. You need it a lot more than—"

She moved closer to him and put her finger to his lips. "I plan on paying back every cent as soon as I get my normal life back."

For some reason neither moved away. Both continued to stare at one another. If she took just one step closer, she'd be able to feel his warm breath on her lips. She knew it, and judging from the look in his eyes, so did he. Leaning in, she waited for him to kiss her.

When he stepped back and walked to the kitchen sink, she was left feeling confused. "Jake?"

He turned slowly to face her, regret written across his face. "I'm a loser, Maddy. As much as I'd love to take you in my arms and drag you up to my bedroom, I respect you way too much to do that."

"You're not a loser," she protested.

He looked away but not before she saw the longing in his eyes. "I come with a lot of baggage. I've been able to handle it up to now by drowning it in booze, but these past few days have made me realize I don't want to do that any—"

"I can help," she interrupted.

A slow smile crossed his face. "Without a doubt, but unfortunately, these are demons I have to slay by myself. After my partner was killed, my commanding officer insisted I see a department therapist, but I wasn't ready then. Now I think I might be."

She knew he was right, and she hated it. And what was she thinking, anyway? Her heart assured her that if he hadn't walked away from her moments before, there was no doubt she would've ended up naked in his bed. And although she suspected it would have surpassed her wildest fantasies, the euphoria would be short-lived. The man had issues, but so did she. First and foremost, she had a murder charge hanging over her head, and if things went terribly wrong, she could end up spending the rest of her life in jail.

She shook her head to chase away that thought. "Jessie will miss you," she said simply.

"Not nearly as much as I'm going to miss her." He paused before adding, "And you, too."

She smiled. "San Antonio is only four hours away."

"And the drive through the small towns between here and there is full of great scenery." He winked. "You may be sorry you opened that door."

"*You* may be sorry you didn't drag me up to your bedroom when you had the chance."

He threw back his head and laughed out loud. "I already am, but I have a nine o'clock meeting with the good sheriff, and I get the sense he doesn't like me already. Imagine how he would feel about me if he knew I'd just finished ravaging his sister-in-law."

"Now you're making me sorry." She laughed before glancing at the clock over the sink. "Oh Lord, Kate will be here in ten minutes, and I haven't even showered."

"Another girly afternoon planned?"

Her eyes turned serious, the light bantering between the two of them over. "Today, I'm hoping to get a lead on the real killer."

"I know there's nothing I can say to stop you from doing that, so I'll just warn you to be careful. There are a lot of bad people out there who don't like being reminded of it."

"I will. I promise. Good luck with Colt today." She hurried out of the room before she tried to change his mind and dragged him to *her* bedroom.

Kate arrived ten minutes late which allowed Maddy enough time to get ready. Dressed in her usual jeans and T-shirt, Kate looked normal again with her hair in a ponytail and sporting just a slight touch of lip gloss. Jake was still up in his room when they left, and she was glad of that. She wasn't ready to tell her younger sister about what had almost happened in the kitchen earlier, because it was probably nothing. Although she hoped she was wrong about that, she mentally scolded herself for acting like a teenage girl.

"Did you call the Dallas guy?" Kate asked as they climbed into Maddy's car.

Maddy nodded. "Yeah. Got the number from a Google search and left a voicemail. Told him we'd be stopping by after lunch to discuss a delicate matter."

"Jeez, Maddy! Get right to the point, why don't you? What makes you think he'll be at home this afternoon? What if he's on a business trip or something?"

"I thought about that, but I still want to go to his house. Sometimes seeing how someone lives speaks louder than actually having a conversation with that person. Even better if his wife is there and we get a look at her." She glanced quickly at her sister. "You used to be the adventurous one, Katie. Since when did you become such a worry wart?"

"Since Lainey almost got herself killed last year trying to find Tessa's killer. Colt warned us that people get bent out of shape when they think you're asking the wrong questions."

"Oh, pfft!" Maddy maneuvered the car off the freeway at Oak Lawn and headed toward downtown Dallas. "If you see someplace that looks interesting, let me know. I'm starving."

Her stomach was noisily telling her she should have eaten more than a piece of toast that morning with Jake and Jessie.

"What about over there?" Kate pointed to a small restaurant tucked between two tall buildings. "The Gypsy Café. I think I read about this place in the fine dining section of the Sunday newspaper."

"Is it expensive?" Maddy pulled into a slot in the front and turned off the engine.

Kate made a wiggling motion with her hand. "Middle of the road. The article said the food was excellent, though. Come on. We'll split something." She opened her door and climbed out of the car, speaking over the hood. "Think of it as an adventure. I'll even spring since I just got paid and have a little spare cash."

"You're treating? Now I'm really concerned about you," Maddy teased. "Okay, you've sold me. Let's go find out what all the hoopla is about."

The maître d' approached them almost as soon as they walked through the door. He led them to a cozy table near the window where they could see the Dallas skyline. Ten minutes later, they were enjoying the best chicken salad sandwich Maddy had ever tasted, making her wish she hadn't agreed to half it with her sister.

When she shoved the last bite into her mouth, she glanced at Kate. "Since you generously sprang for the sandwich, I'll do dessert."

She scanned the restaurant for the waiter so they could get a look at the dessert menu. Just when she was about to give up, she located him at the other side of the restaurant.

Before she could get his attention, her eyes settled on a man sitting at a corner table holding hands with a sexy redhead. He was laughing at something the woman had said, and Maddy was shocked when she recognized him immediately.

"Oh my God!"

"What!" Kate asked, following Maddy's eyes to the table across the way. "You gotta be kidding me? Tell me that's not Deena's husband sitting close enough to that woman to check her pulse without using his fingers."

"That slimy bastard. Come on, Kate, we're going over there."

Maddy stood and headed in that direction with her cell phone in hand and her sister right behind her. She had no idea what she'd say to Mike Hernandez, but she wasn't about to let him think his little tryst was still a secret. As they approached the table, he looked up and immediately she snapped a picture on her phone. She got another one when his expression went from a huge smile that smacked of shared intimacy with the woman to jaw-dropping surprise in a nanosecond. He released the woman's hands as if they were on fire.

"Hello, Mike. Care to introduce us to your lady friend?"

By now he had recovered enough from his initial shock, and he moved into damage control mode. "It isn't what you think, Maddy. She's an associate of mine from work."

Kate stepped forward. "And do you hold hands over lunch with all your associates?" When he didn't respond, she turned to the woman who had yet to utter one word. "Are you aware this man is married?"

The woman glared before finding her voice. "Now that would be none of your business."

"You're a slimeball, Mike, and you always have been. My sister deserves so much better than you." Maddy held up her phone and took a close up of the redhead before grabbing Kate's arm. "Come on. All of a sudden I've lost my appetite for sweets. Let's let our loser brother-in-law finish up with his Jezebel." Still trembling with anger, she guided Kate back to the table.

After they paid the bill and were back in the car, Kate turned to her. "Are we going to tell Deena?"

Maddy sighed. This was one job she didn't want, but as not only Deena's sister but also as her best friend, she had to be the one to do it. "I'll go over there and talk to her tonight."

"For once, I'm glad I have to go to work," Kate said. "Tell her I love her, will you?"

Maddy nodded. "Okay, now let's go visit Francis Montero and get this over with."

Using the car's GPS they found the house easily enough. Although it wasn't in the best neighborhood, Maddy felt safe, especially since the forty-five was tucked away in her purse. Montero lived in a small but well-kept house surrounded by a chain-link fence. After climbing the steps and ringing the doorbell three times, they were about to give up when the door flew open and they came face-to-face with a heavyset Hispanic woman.

"We're from the Census Bureau," Maddy lied. "We need to talk to Francis Montero." She hoped the woman wouldn't ask for their credentials.

"He's not here," she answered in broken English.

"When do you expect him back?"

"Never, if I'm lucky," the woman said, defiantly. "He lives with his mother now."

Maddy studied her face, trying to figure out if the anger had anything to do with Chrissy's pictures. But there was no way of knowing that, short of outright asking. She wasn't ready to do that yet. "Do you have his mother's address?"

The woman turned and disappeared for a few minutes. When she returned she handed Maddy a sticky note with an address scribbled on it. Then without another word she shut the door in their faces.

"That went well," Kate said. "You think she knows about the pictures?"

"I have no idea." Maddy put the address into her GPS. "It's on the other side of the city. If we go there now, we'll get stuck in traffic on the way home." She punched in her home address and started the engine. "I'll come back tomorrow to have a chat with him and his mom. Besides, you have to be at work at four, and I have to go see Deena. I can't let her go another night without knowing."

Neither sister had much to say on the ride home. Immersed in her own thoughts, Maddy was already searching her brain for a way to soften the blow when she told her sister about her jerk of a husband. The only good thing was that this wouldn't come as a total shock to Deena since she'd already found evidence that the rat was cheating.

By the time they arrived back at Maddy's house and Kate had left for the hospital in her own car, Maddy had already formulated a plan. Deena got off work at five, and she'd called ahead and left a message telling her she'd be at her house at five-thirty with burgers.

She had a little time before Jessie got home from school, and she decided to do some research on her computer about Agostinelli and Nicky Cavicchia, the mobster from New York. When she researched him on the Internet, she found a boatload of articles written about the impending trial, and quickly, she was immersed in reading them. She was particularly interested in a New York Times post that had gone into detail about the history of the Cavicchia family, as far back as the nineteen hundreds.

She was about to shut down the computer and wait for her daughter on the porch when she spotted a familiar face in one of the pictures with Nicky Cavicchia. She leaned in closer to the screen for a better look. It was a picture of a triumphant Cavicchia and his lawyer leaving the New York City courthouse after one of his many trials.

But Nicky Cavicchia wasn't the one who had caught her attention. Standing beside him, dressed in a dark blue suit, was his lawyer, a man who looked almost identical to someone who had recently come into Maddy's life. When she spotted his name, she nearly threw up. The article went on to say that the lawyer had later been convicted of tax evasion and had gone to federal prison where he'd died less than a year later of lung cancer. His name was Mario Pirelli, and he'd left a wife and two young sons, Anthony and Giovanni.

Holy crap! Her lawyer was the son of Nicky Cavicchia's former counsel.

After she recovered from the initial shock, she began to see things clearer. It all made sense now why he'd taken her on as a client for a fraction of his usual fees.

The man was probably on the Cavicchia payroll and was being paid to make sure she went to jail for the murder of Joey Agostinelli. A murder Cavicchia himself had probably orchestrated.

She picked up the phone to call Colt and tell him what she'd discovered when Jessie walked through the door. She remembered what she still had to do at Deena's house. Tomorrow was soon enough to divulge her new information. Besides, she couldn't prove any of her suspicions yet, but she fully intended to investigate further to find out why the son of the former consigliere for the head of a New York mob family had agreed to represent her.

Coincidence? She thought not, but it would have to wait. Right now she had an unpleasant job to do.

After giving her daughter a coupon and a twenty-dollar bill, she instructed her to order pizza for her and Jake. She was more than a little disappointed that the night had turned out like this instead of the way she'd planned. Since this was Jake's last night in Vineyard, she'd hoped the three of them could go someplace nice and eat. But telling her sister about Mike was a priority now. She'd have to say her goodbyes to Jake the next morning.

When Deena opened the door, she took one look at Maddy before her brows drew together with worry. "Please tell me nothing's happened to Mom."

Maddy shook her head. "I brought food. Do you want to eat first then make us an Irish coffee while we talk?"

"Oh boy, this must really be bad if you're here by yourself and think I need a drink." She shook her head. "As much as I love food, there's no way I can eat right now until you tell me why you're here. My imagination is going crazy."

Maddy set the bag on the table and walked over to Deena's coffee pot. "Okay, we'll do the food later, but we need the drink now."

When both of them had a steaming cup of coffee in front of them with a healthy dollop of Irish whiskey in each, Maddy reached across the kitchen table and grabbed Deena's hand. "I would rather pull my fingernails out one by one than to have to tell you this, Deena."

"Oh dear God, Maddy, spit it out before I pull your fingernails out myself."

"Kate and I stopped at an out-of-the-way restaurant near downtown Dallas today," she began, praying for a delicate way to say it. But there was no easy way. "We saw Mike having lunch with another woman."

Deena thought about that for a while, and then laughed. "He takes his clients out to lunch all the time." She blew out a relieved breath. "For a while there you had me more than a little worried, Maddy."

Maddy couldn't let her sister believe his lies anymore, but for some reason, she held back on showing her the photos she'd taken. They could use them if divorce proceedings got ugly, but now wasn't the time. "This was no client relationship kind of lunch, Deena. I'm sorry. His hands were all over her, and she basically admitted they were having an affair."

Okay maybe she hadn't exactly admitted it, but their body language had spoken volumes.

"I know you mean well, Maddy, but before I go jumping off the deep end, I need to talk to Mike about this."

"I understand," Maddy said. "I just thought you'd want to know what we saw today."

"And I appreciate your telling me, but I've been married to the man for a long time. I know he's had affairs in the past, but yesterday when I said I was sick and tired of his womanizing ways, I was just angry." She turned away so Maddy wouldn't see the tears. "I have to give him the benefit of the doubt. He's all I've got."

Before Maddy could respond, the doorbell rang. Deena jumped up and ran in that direction, and Maddy followed right behind her. When she opened the door, Maddy gasped in surprise at seeing Colt on the front steps. Her first thought was that somehow he'd found out what she'd been up to and was here to read her the riot act and probably fire her. But as soon as she saw the way he was looking at Deena, she began to worry that it was something more.

"Colt, what are you doing here?" Deena asked. "If you're looking for Lainey, she's at home."

The sadness in his eyes was evident when he shook his head. "I'm here on official business, Deena."

She covered her mouth with her hand but not before her breath hitched. "What's the matter?"

"I just got a call that a body was found in an empty field on the outskirts of town. I sent Flanagan and Rogers to investigate." He paused and gathered his sister-in-law in his arms. "It's Mike, Deena. He's dead."

Chapter Twenty-two

"How did he die?" Deena asked after her sobs slowed to an occasional hiccup.

"He was shot," Colt said softly, still holding his sister-in-law in his arms. "We'll know more after the autopsy. By then the crime scene guys will have had an opportunity to take a look at the evidence they processed at the scene." He massaged the back of Deena's head, probably exactly the same way he did to his own daughter when she was hurting. "I'm so sorry, Deena."

"When do you think we can have the funeral, Colt?" Deena's face still registered the shock she was feeling as she caught her breath. "I have no idea what to do next."

Maddy moved in and took her from her brother-in-law. "Don't worry about that, honey. That's what families are for."

"I know you think he deserved this, Maddy, but—"

"Shh." Maddy pulled her sister closer. "No one deserves to die like that. And for the record, I always tried to see the good in Mike."

Deena nodded, sniffing back more tears. She looked up at Colt. "Why would someone kill him?"

"We don't know, but we're going to find out. I promise." He reached into his pocket and pulled out a clear plastic evidence bag with Mike's phone inside. Maneuvering the keypad through the plastic, he pulled up the latest entries and showed them to Deena, pointing to one in particular. "You recognize this number?"

"No. Should I?"

He shrugged. "I was hoping you might. Seems Mike called it several times today. According to the coroner's best estimate, once right before the time of his murder."

Deena made eye contact with Maddy. "Let me see it again." After taking another look, she glanced up at Colt and blew out a breath. "This may be the number of the woman Mike was seeing on the side."

It was no secret to anyone in the family that Mike Hernandez had cheated on Deena many times over the years. To Colt's credit, he acted like his brother-in-law's indiscretions were not old news. "What makes you think that, Deena?"

Once again Deena stole a look Maddy's way. After Maddy nodded, she said, "Maddy and Kate saw him with another woman today at a restaurant near downtown Dallas."

Colt twisted toward Maddy. "What were you two doing downtown today?"

"I had an appointment with my lawyer, and Kate had the afternoon off and graciously offered to keep me company. We had lunch at the Gypsy Café on McKinney Avenue and Mike was there with a sexy..." She stopped abruptly before continuing, "With a redhead."

"Did he see you?"

"Oh yeah. We marched over to his table and confronted him. He said she was a client, but we all knew it was more intimate than that."

Colt pulled out a notebook. "Had you ever seen this woman before?" When Maddy shook her head, he continued, "And this was what time today?"

"About one. We didn't stay very long because we had another stop—" She caught her breath. She had been so close to blurting out that they hadn't stayed long so that they could run by Francis Montero's house before heading back to Vineyard. She hoped Colt hadn't picked up on the near slip.

No such luck.

"Another stop?"

She shifted her weight to the other foot, hoping he couldn't read her mind the way he always seemed to do. He was more like a brother to her than an in-law, and he could usually tell when she was lying. "Kate wanted to go to one of the outlet stores on Harry Hines Boulevard to look for leather purses. Since she had to be back at the hospital by four, we were in somewhat of a hurry."

Colt's stare was so intense, it nearly caused her to crumble under the scrutiny. There was no way she wanted him to find out the real reason she and Kate had gone into Dallas that afternoon. Not if she wanted to keep her job.

Apparently her explanation appeased him, and he turned back to Deena. "Do you happen to have a list of Mike's clients here?"

"No, but I'm sure his secretary can get that for you." Deena sat down at the table. "You think this woman had something to do with his death?"

"I don't know, but I'd like to talk to her to see if there might be a jealous husband in the picture. It sounds like she may have been one of the last people to see him alive."

Just then the door opened and Lainey rushed through. As soon as she spied Deena sitting at the kitchen table, she ran to her. Immediately, she enveloped her in her arms, causing more tears from both of them.

While his wife comforted Deena, Colt closed his notebook and faced Maddy. "I'm going to let you women take care of your sister, but if either you or she remembers anything at all that might help us identify this other woman, give me a call. In the meantime, if it's okay with you, Deena, I'll send Flanagan over to go through Mike's personal belongings to see if he can find anything that might help us identify her or anyone else who might have had a problem with him."

When she nodded, he walked over and kissed the top of her head. "Like I said, we'll find whoever did this to Mike. I promise." After a quick peck on his wife's cheek, he made his way to the door.

Maddy stopped him before he got there. "I need to talk to you." When he looked confused, she lowered her voice. No sense alarming her sisters, especially now that Deena already had so much on her mind. "I found something on the Internet that was pretty disturbing."

"About Mike's murder?"

She shook her head. "About my case. I was surfing the Net reading all I could on Agostinelli, and I found an article in the New York Times about Nicky Cavicchia."

Colt widened eyes showed his interest. "We found his wife's necklace, you know."

"Jake told me. But back to my research, you're never going to believe who the lead counsel for Cavicchia was before going off to prison himself for tax evasion."

Now she really had his attention. He grabbed her elbow, guiding her away from the door and farther from Lainey and Deena. "I have no idea, but why is this important?"

"Because up until eight years ago, the consigliere of the Cavicchia family was none other than Mario Pirelli, the father of the man defending me for Agostinelli's murder."

She didn't have to wait long for his reaction. His narrowed eyes and the scowl hinted that he was thinking the same thing she was. "You're sure?"

"Positive. Apparently Mario died not long after he'd gone to prison, and his obituary listed Anthony Pirelli as one of his sons."

A slight grin tipped the corners of Colt's mouth. "Great catch, Maddy. Now that's the kind of detective work you can do for yourself without getting into trouble." He walked to the door and stepped out before turning back. "I think it's about time I had another talk with your lawyer."

She smiled to herself, glad she hadn't had to fess up that she wasn't being the good girl he hoped she was. It was crucial that he believed that. She had one more angle to check out before she could just sit back and wait for a jury of her peers to tell her she didn't kill Agostinelli.

Tomorrow, first thing after Jake left the house, she'd head into Dallas again to try to talk to Francis Montero. He'd probably deny having any contact with Chrissy, but she'd grown very good at reading people. She'd just watch Montero's face when she showed him the picture.

Surprise reactions always spoke volumes.

* * * * *

The next morning as Maddy and Deena sat around the kitchen table drinking their coffee, they made plans to meet with a mortuary director. Hopefully, the M.E. would be finished with the autopsy on Mike's body by then, and they could go forward with the funeral arrangements.

Maddy had insisted that Deena spend the night with her, and they'd stayed up late reminiscing about Mike. She'd let Deena talk it out, mostly about all the good memories she'd had with him. Maddy couldn't help wondering why people never remembered the bad things that happened in a relationship when someone died. To hear Deena talk, Mike had been a saint. But she hadn't stopped her sister or said anything negative, believing this was what Deena needed right now to get through the next few days.

Jake had come back to the house just before dinner, and when he'd heard about Mike, he'd insisted on cooking his mother's spaghetti and meatballs recipe again. Several of Deena's neighbors had found out that she was at Maddy's house and had stopped by with dessert and condolences. With all the company and distractions, Deena had loosened up and even laughed out loud a couple of times. But Maddy knew today's events would be hard on her.

Jake wondered into the kitchen just as Maddy stood to pour a second cup for herself and Deena. After parking his luggage in a corner, he squeezed Deena's shoulder on his way to the coffee pot.

"How are you doing today?"

She shrugged. "Truthfully, I'm better, but I'm not looking forward to the trip to the funeral home to pick out a coffin." She took a sip of the steaming liquid. "I was finally able to reach Mike's sister late last night, and she's going to inform the rest of his family."

"What about his parents?" Jake took a seat beside her.

"They're gone. Mike was a change of life baby, and they died before he graduated from high school. His two older sisters basically raised him. Through the years, though, he drifted away from them over one incident or another. I was afraid they might not come to his funeral."

"And are they?"

She nodded. "At least his oldest sister said she was. I'm not sure about the other one."

"When did you say you're meeting with the funeral director?" Maddy asked, topping off both Deena's and Jake's cup with the last of the pot.

"At two." Deena looked up. "You're still going with me, right?"

"Absolutely. I would never let you do this by yourself." She glanced at her watch. "I have something to do this morning, so I'll drop you off at your house. Then I'll pick you up around one."

"Where are you going?" Deena asked, leaning forward.

Maddy wasn't sure she wanted Jake to know she hadn't yet given up sleuthing, even though she'd promised she would. He'd probably echo Colt's warnings that it was too dangerous.

Her plans today only included talking to an old lady and her son. How dangerous could that be, especially since she'd have her husband's forty-five with her?

"Well, where are you going?" Jake asked, eyeing her suspiciously.

She decided to come clean. "To pay a visit to a man I believe was being blackmailed by Chrissy Rockford and Agostinelli."

"Does the sheriff know?" Jake asked.

"No. He'd only try to talk me out of it."

"With good reason," Jake said, still boring a hole into her with his stare.

"I want to go with you," Deena said, suddenly. When Maddy didn't respond, she pleaded. "Please, Maddy, I'll go crazy sitting home by myself trying to smile every time one of my well-meaning neighbors drops by with food that will probably never get eaten."

"Are you sure you're up to it?"

Deena's eyes lit up. "It will keep my mind off everything else. I didn't get to go with you and Kate yesterday, and now it's my turn to have fun." Her eyes turned defiant. "It's probably a good thing I wasn't with you and Kate yesterday.

If I'd seen my husband with that woman, I might have killed the lying bastard myself right there in the restaurant."

Maddy couldn't help it and laughed out loud. "Guess this is what they call the angry stage of grieving."

"Damn straight," Deena said. "I loved Mike more than life itself, but it's time I took off the blinders. The kindest thing I can say about him right now is that he was not a model husband."

"Well, it sounds like you ladies have your entire day planned, so I'll just say goodbye and get on my way," Jake said after he chugged the last of his coffee.

For a minute, Maddy had forgotten that today was the day he was heading back to San Antonio. "Jessie and I will miss you," she said, honestly.

She really would miss talking to him around the kitchen table. And for the past few days she hadn't had to nag her daughter to get her homework done. Jessie knew Maddy would never let her stay up with her and Jake if she hadn't finished her school work.

"Me too," Deena said. "And tell your mom I said her son can cook for me anytime."

He grinned. "Will do." He stood and carried his empty cup to the sink. After rinsing it and placing it into the dishwasher, he turned back to Maddy. "Where did you say this guy lives?"

"On Grand Avenue near Fair Park. Why?"

"Just curious. That's a rough part of town. You and Deena need to keep your eyes open." He grabbed his luggage and headed for the door.

Maddy followed behind. Before he walked out, he bent down and kissed her cheek. "Thanks for everything. I hope you were serious about taking a drive to San Antonio real soon."

"As serious as a heart attack. There's something about you that I find intriguing under that bad boy exterior, Jake Matthews, and I'm determined to discover what that something is."

This time his grin covered his entire face. "I hope you won't be disappointed." He walked down the driveway to his car, turning one last time to wave goodbye.

You should never have let him go.

Maddy was surprised to see Tessa beside her. "What could I have done? Locked him in his room?"

For starters, yes. A man like that needs a reason to stay. Captivity works as well as anything, I guess.

"Are you talking to Tessa?" Deena asked.

"Yes."

Tell Deena I wish I could hug her.

Maddy repeated Tessa's words to her sister.

"I know she would if she could. Say what you want about the Garcia girls, but we stick together, no matter how much we fight." Deena turned to the sink. "I love you, Tessa."

Don't bother telling her I'm right next to her, Tessa said. *So what are we doing today?*

"Going to Dallas to confront a possible killer."

That's just the kind of thing I need to do to make me forget how dead I really am.

* * * * *

The ride to Dallas took longer than Maddy expected due to construction in the canyon near downtown. It was already after ten when they pulled up to the curb at the address Francis Montero's wife had given them the day before.

I'm wondering why anyone could possibly believe this guy has enough money to pay a blackmailer, Tessa said. *This house is a dump.*

"Don't be so quick to judge," Maddy said, before repeating Tessa's words to Deena.

"She's right. It is pretty bad," Deena said, glancing around as she got out of the car in front of the house. "Are you sure this is the right address?"

Maddy checked the card with the address once again. "Yep. Like I said, this doesn't mean Montero doesn't have money. His wife kicked him out, remember? This is his mother's house, and I'll bet she's lived here all her life."

"Was his house in any better shape?"

Maddy thought for a moment. "Not much. Tessa may have a point."

Walking up the porch steps, Maddy nearly tripped over a loose board. After the second knock, the door swung open, and they were greeted by the shortest Hispanic woman Maddy had ever seen.

"Are you Mrs. Montero?" Maddy began, checking out the woman as she spoke. Standing about five feet tall with dark hair pulled back into a bun, the overweight woman looked off-balance as she held onto the doorjamb.

"Yes. And who might you be?"

"I'm Madelyn Castillo, and this is my sister Deena. We work for the Census Bureau, and we need to speak to your son Francis."

A look of surprise, then anguish, crossed the woman's face. "Junior isn't here right now."

"Junior is Francis Montero?"

The woman nodded. "His daddy was Francis Senior." She sighed. "I'm sorry I can't help you, but I have no idea when he'll be back."

She was about to close the door when Maddy stuck her foot inside to stop her. "You can answer the questions for him. May we come in?"

When the woman hesitated, Maddy added, "It's urgent that we get your son's records completed as soon as possible. It may affect his income tax return this year." She crossed her fingers behind her back, hoping that lying to this woman wouldn't be judged too harshly up above.

Mrs. Montero opened the door and motioned for them to come in. Once inside, she directed them to the small living room off to the right. Both Maddy and Deena took a seat on what looked to be a brand-new leather couch.

Tessa flopped down between them. *So, it's true. You should never judge a book by its cover,* she said, putting her nose next to the leather and sniffing. *This is the good stuff.*

"How can I help you?" the woman asked, sitting down in the matching leather chair opposite them.

"Mrs. Montero, do you—"

"Call me Alicia," she interrupted.

Maddy smiled. This might be easier than she thought. "Alicia, do you know if your son was having financial problems lately?" She held her breath. No way a Census Bureau employee would be asking that kind of question. She hoped Alicia didn't know this.

The woman never blinked. "Junior was always having money problems of some kind."

"Is that why he lives with you?" Deena asked, scooting forward on the couch.

Alicia looked surprised by the question. "That's part of the reason. He and his wife separated a while back, and Junior's been here with me ever since."

"When do you expect him back? I'd really like to talk to him," Maddy said.

The older woman's eyes turned sad, and she swallowed before speaking. "I don't know."

The detective in Maddy immediately made note of the way the woman had lowered her eyes and picked at her fingernails. Alicia Montero was lying, but why?

She decided to be blunt. "Was your son being blackmailed, Alicia?"

You always were as subtle as a jackhammer, Tessa teased. *I used to...Oh my God!*

"What?" Maddy said, before she remembered that no one else could hear Tessa.

Look over there. Tessa pointed to the mantle above the fireplace.

There in the center was a colorful insulated lunch bag, exactly like the one Mike had used to bring Thanksgiving leftovers to the police station the night Agostinelli was killed. The one that was nowhere to be found when they'd looked for it a few days ago.

Was it a coincidence there was an identical one in the house of a man who very well might be Agostinelli's killer?

Before Maddy had a chance to ask about it, the front door opened and a well-dressed Hispanic man walked in.

"Hello, Mrs. Castillo," he said with a look so evil that Maddy shuddered.

Maddy looked confused. If she had met the attractive man before, surely she would have remembered. "I'm sorry. Do I know you?"

Although he was still smiling, there was no glee in his eyes. "Not personally, but I'm sure you'll remember Greta."

A woman stepped from behind him and walked into the living room. Dressed in a pair of jeans so tight they could have been sprayed on and a sweater that showed off her generous assets, the attractive redhead smiled.

"She knows me as Jezebel."

For the first time since Agostinelli's murder, Maddy felt a ripple of fear course through her body, and she cursed herself for not heeding Colt's warning to stay out of the investigation.

She racked her brain to come up with a reason why the woman she'd seen having lunch with Mike yesterday, just hours before his death, would be standing in front of her right now.

The only thing that popped into her brain was a red flag, and she gripped her purse with the weapon.

She and her sister were in big trouble.

Chapter Twenty-three

"Eduardo, do you know these women from the Census Bureau?" Alicia Montero asked her son.

His eyes turned cold. "Is that what they told you, Mama?" When she nodded, he huffed. "They lied to you so you'd let them into your house. They're here to rob you—or worse."

"That's not true." Maddy attempted to get up from the couch before the redhead shoved her back down with enough force to jar her entire body. She turned to Alicia. "It's true. We're not from the Census Bureau, but we didn't come to steal from you. I'm a cop, and this is my sister Deena. We came to see Francis—Junior—to find out if he was being blackmailed by a man who was killed in a jail cell under my watch last week."

Alicia's eyes widened. "Why would you think Junior was being blackmailed? He left over two weeks ago, and I haven't heard from him since." The sadness in Alicia's eyes was hard to miss.

Maddy blew out a frustrated breath. If what his mother said was true, there was no way the man could've killed Agostinelli. She was back to square one again.

"What makes you think Junior was being squeezed?" Eddie Montero asked, before moving to the chair beside his mother and sitting down.

Maddy debated whether to tell him about the picture, then decided if she could get this man to understand why she and her sister has shown up on his mother's doorstep asking questions, maybe he'd let them leave without an incident. She promised herself if she and Deena made it back to Vineyard, she'd give up nosing around in the investigation and leave it up to Colt and her buddies at the police station to clear her name.

When she picked up her purse to show him the picture, both Eddie and the redhead reacted. Greta reached her first and snatched it from her hands. Quickly, she opened it and searched. A smile spread across her face when she pulled out Robbie's forty-five.

"And what do we have here?" Greta twirled the gun in her fingers before pointing it at Maddy's head. After a minute she lowered it and stepped closer to Alicia to show her the weapon. "Eddie was right, Alicia. They were going to rob you."

"No, we weren't," Maddy argued. "They're the ones lying to you."

Greta spun around and slammed the gun into the side of Maddy's face, causing her to fall sideways into Deena. She moaned as the pain made her lightheaded. Deena immediately wrapped her arm around her to keep her from falling any farther.

"Greta, what in the hell do you think you're doing?" Alicia shouted. "Put that gun down now."

Greta made eye contact with Eddie. When he nodded she walked over to the fireplace and laid the weapon on the mantle next to the lunch bag.

Maddy knew right then that the older woman had at least some influence over both her son and the woman. She decided to use that to her advantage. "Alicia, Deena and I are convinced that Junior didn't have anything to do with killing the man in Vineyard last week. So, if it's okay with you, we'll just get out of your way and let you visit with your son."

"Not so fast," Eddie said, jumping up from the chair. "You still haven't told me why you thought my brother was being blackmailed."

"I tried to do that, but your girlfriend grabbed my purse, remember? I have a picture of him in there."

Eddie scowled. "That's impossible."

Maddy forced herself to stay calm. There was a very real possibility that either Eddie or Greta—or both—had murdered her brother-in-law. But if she and Deena were going to get out of this house alive, she'd have to pretend that thought had never entered her mind.

Eddie reached for the purse Greta still held in her hands and rifled through it before handing it back to Maddy. "Show me."

She dug for her cell phone, wondering if she could hit the speed dial number and call the Vineyard Police Station before she pulled it out of her purse. But Eddie must have been thinking the same thing. He reached in and ripped it from her hand before she had a chance to do anything with it.

"Where is it?" he asked, impatiently.

"Click on the photo icon," she answered, bummed that he'd thwarted her attempt to call for help. She didn't have a backup plan.

Quickly, he scrolled through the pictures until he found the one he was looking for. After studying it for a few minutes, he looked up. "Where did you get this? I have the originals and all the negatives."

A shiver ran up Maddy's spine as she realized the meaning of what he had just said. The only way he could have them in his possession was if he had stolen them from Chrissy Rockford's purse. It also meant he'd probably killed her. She shifted nervously on the couch. The situation was dire and growing more critical by the second. She had to think of some way to get out of there with Deena, but at the moment, she was coming up blank.

She decided to be honest with the man. "I found these in the purse of the woman having sex with your brother. I took a snapshot with my phone."

"And when exactly was that?"

She wondered why that was important. "The day before she was murdered."

He stood directly in front of her. "There was a small notebook in the woman's purse along with these pictures. Did you take that, too?"

So it was his book she'd found. That's probably why he'd torn Chrissy's apartment to pieces before he'd killed her.

Maddy shuddered, thinking if she hadn't taken the book, if Chrissy could have handed it over to Montero, she would still be alive today. Then she realized that Chrissy had been a dead woman from the very moment Eddie walked into her apartment, just like she and Deena would be if she told them where she'd stashed the book. It was her only leverage with him.

"I never saw a notebook," she lied.

He studied her eyes, and then suddenly belted her across the face, sending her once again to the back of the couch.

Alicia jumped up and slapped her son's face. "You will not hurt this woman in my house. Do you hear me?" Before he had a chance to respond, she lashed out at him again. "You were always cruel, especially to your older brother. I tried so many times to get your worthless father to take you with him when he left, but even he didn't want you. I spent my whole life protecting Junior from becoming just like you."

Maddy watched Montero's eyes turn sad at hearing his mother degrade him like that. Then they reflected a rage so intense, she shivered.

He must have forgotten about her for a moment because he turned to his mother. "You never tried to love me, no matter what I said or did. No matter how many times I saved Junior's sorry ass from one situation or another. He was the one who was worthless. Not me."

"Don't say that about him," she shouted. "I don't know what I did to deserve an evil child like you. When Junior comes home, we never want to see you again. Do you hear me?"

Eddie threw his head back and laughed out loud. "I hear you, Mama, but don't hold your breath waiting for Junior to come home anytime soon. I made sure that wouldn't happen."

Alicia screamed. "What did you do, Eddie?" Tears were already forming in her eyes.

He smirked. "Let's just say he's with the fishes, and leave it at that."

"Oh God, tell me you didn't kill him. What did he ever do to you except love you no matter what?" Her voice pleaded with him to tell her he was lying.

Eddie cocked his head and smirked. "The lady cop's right. Junior was being blackmailed. Seems he was caught on film in a compromising position with a hooker." He tsked. "You remember how hard he was trying to talk Ronda into taking him back after she'd thrown him out the last time? He was afraid if he didn't pay up, they'd send the picture to her like they'd threatened. She would never have allowed him back in her house after that."

"He should have come to me. I would have found a way to give him the money," Alicia said, now sobbing.

Eddie shook his head. "And where would you have gotten it, Mama? What little you get from Social Security doesn't even pay your bills. You would've come to me, and I would've rescued him like I always did."

"Why didn't he go to you for the money?"

Eddie stared down at the floor, almost like a little boy who had to confess to his mother what he'd done. "He did, but only after I caught him trying to steal a huge shipment of drugs from me. When I confronted him and told him I was cutting him off, he lashed out at me. That's when I discovered that somehow he had found my notebook and used it to pay off the blackmailers."

It was all becoming very clear to Maddy. The names she'd seen in the small book were either drug users or people Eddie had on his payroll. Big-time names, that had they been made public, would have ruined a lot of careers. Eddie must have guarded that list like a Rottweiler. No wonder he went berserk when he found out the book was in the hands of someone like Agostinelli.

Eddie noticed that she was deep in concentration. "If you have any idea where that book is, I'd advise you to tell me right now."

Regardless of his menacing attitude, she was positive the book was her ticket out of this jam. If he wanted it badly enough, and he acted like he did, he wouldn't kill them until he had it back in his possession. It gave her a little leeway and more time to try to find a way to escape.

"It might have been in Chrissy's purse when I searched it. But I don't have it with me now."

"She's lying," Greta chimed in from behind the couch. "She's trying to save her ass."

Maddy had almost forgotten the redhead was still there. She turned to look her in the eye. "You should know all about lying. You're a freaking expert at it." Still glaring at her, she said, "Did you know your girlfriend was having an affair with Deena's husband, Eddie?"

Finally she broke eye contact with Greta and looked back at Eddie to see how he had reacted to the news that his girlfriend had cheated on him.

His eyes crinkled with laughter. "For being a cop, you're not very smart. Who do you think put her up to it?"

When Maddy didn't respond he turned to Deena. "Getting your husband to believe a woman like Greta would actually fall for him was like taking candy from a baby. It was even easier to persuade him to drop off Thanksgiving leftovers for you at the police station." He pointed to the lunch container on the mantle, the one Maddy had noticed right before he'd walked in his mother's house. "Say cheese for the camera."

Holy hell! No wonder he'd known every move she'd made the night Agostinelli was killed. Her brother-in-law was not only a womanizer. He may have been an accessory to murder, as well.

"How'd you get the other phone in my desk drawer?" Maddy asked.

"That was the easy part. When you weren't looking, he just slipped it in."

"Was my husband in on the murder, too?" Deena asked leaning forward now.

"He had no idea why I asked him to bring the leftovers or to plant the phone," Greta said, smiling at Deena as if to taunt her. "Your husband was so horny, he would've done anything I asked, plus I slipped him a couple grand. Unfortunately for him, he put two and two together and figured it all out when Bernardi was killed. Then he made the fatal mistake of demanding more money for his silence."

"You're a whore and always will be," Deena said defiantly, staring Greta down before turning back to Alicia. "I'm so sorry for the loss of your son. I can't even imagine how you must feel right now. I wish I could hug you and wipe away your tears."

Alicia nodded as the tears continued to streak down her face. Maddy could see her heart was breaking, knowing that the son she despised had killed the one she'd adored. But it was just like Deena with her heart of gold to empathize with the woman whose son had also had a part in her own husband's death.

"How long did it take you to plan the murder so that it would fall on me?" Maddy asked.

She had to keep him talking until she figured out how to save their lives. Her eyes wandered toward the mantle, and she pretended to look at the lunch container. Her gun was at the other end of the wooden shelf, closer to Eddie and his mother than to her. If she went for it, she'd never make it.

Eddie followed her eyes before responding. "I couldn't believe how everything just fell into place. We set Foxworthy up to be a blackmail victim and paid him to start the fight at the bar that night. We knew Bernardi was a hothead and would take the bait. With Greta masquerading as you in a uniform and a dark wig and Foxworthy positively identifying you, you looked guilty as hell. It was genius, don't you think?"

Maddy thought about this for a minute. "How did you know I'd be on duty that night instead of Flanagan?" Things would have been very different if he'd been there. Or would they have shown up at his house instead of hers, with a gun to his kid's head?

"You underestimate me, my dear. Who do you think arranged for Flanagan's ex to win a three-day trip to Bermuda for that weekend only?"

Maddy bit her lower lip. He had thought of everything, including getting Flanagan's wife out of town. He'd obviously done his homework on all of them and knew how it would play out. Their only chance of surviving now was to convince him that she indeed had the book he wanted so badly. But she still had unanswered questions. "Why did you kill Foxworthy if he was in on it with you?"

He smiled at Greta. "My girl here got a little too aggressive with your gun. She was supposed to aim higher and only nick him, not put a hole in his gut. The asshole demanded more money because of it." He waved his hand in the air. "He found out the hard way that nobody threatens Eddie Montero."

Maddy stopped listening after the first sentence, and her mind raced. She swiveled to face the redhead. "So it really was you who killed Bernardo? And by the way, his real name was Joey Agostinelli. He was in Vineyard after he slipped away from protective custody in New Jersey. Seems he was a mob informant and pissed off a lot of bad guys. Had you waited a few more days, they probably would've taken care of him for you."

"But I needed the notebook back."

"That's why you killed him?"

Eddie nodded. "The coward cried like a girl before he gave it up. Told Greta his girlfriend had it, but she got a little trigger-happy before he had a chance to give up her name. I thought all was lost. Lucky for me, you led me right to her."

"Me?" Maddy was already trying to remember the day she and Lainey talked to Chrissy Rockford. That was the only time she'd had contact with the blonde. Eddie must have been following them. What kind of cop was she that she hadn't even noticed?

"Yeah. Some cop you are," he said as if he reading her mind. "But the slut didn't have my book. The only possible explanation was that someone had taken it from her purse." His eyes grew angry. "I figured that someone had to have been you. Imagine my surprise when I saw you sitting in my mother's living room." He pointed to the lunch container camera on the mantel before charging the couch.

Maddy braced herself for another assault.

Before she could react, the loud boom of a gunshot echoed in the tiny room. Immediately, she felt the full weight of Eddie Montero's body as he fell onto her, blood streaming from a hole in his chest.

Chapter Twenty-four

"No!" Greta screamed, running from the back of the couch to the front and pulling Eddie off Maddy's body. "Oh God, no."

Maddy glanced in the direction of where the shot had been fired. Apparently, no one had noticed when Alicia Montero had casually gotten out of her chair and walked over to the fireplace. Now, she stood holding the smoking gun that had just killed her son. For a split second, Maddy thought she saw the corner of Alicia's mouth tip in a smile.

Then Greta lowered Eddie's body to the floor and lunged at Alicia, knocking her back into the fireplace and sending Maddy's gun skittering across the floor. Before Maddy could get up and step around the body to keep Greta from beating the older woman to a pulp, Deena jumped up, grabbed a lamp from the end table, and cold cocked the crazed redhead.

"That's for Mike," she said simply.

Quickly, Maddy ran to her gun which had ended up on the floor behind the couch. Certain neither Eddie nor Greta would be a threat to them anytime soon, she picked it up and walked to the wall phone and dialed 911.

Within minutes, the place was crawling with emergency technicians and Dallas police officers. Other than a huge goose egg on the back of Alicia's head and a large cut over her eye where Greta had landed a right hook, the elderly woman was okay. Deena had immediately knelt down on the floor next to her to wait for help to arrive, and now reluctantly allowed the EMTs to move her to a gurney. Greta was still unconscious from the hit she'd taken and was loaded onto another one.

"Thank you for saving our lives," Maddy said, squeezing Alicia's hand for a quick second as they carried her past.

"I'm sorry," the woman whispered before they lifted her into the ambulance.

Maddy hugged Deena while more cops filed into the house. She looked up, sure she was dreaming when she saw Jake standing in the doorway. He rushed over and enveloped both her and her sister in his arms.

"How'd you get here?" she asked, not really caring. The fact that he was there was all that mattered.

He brushed back a lock of her hair that had fallen across her face. "I made it all the way to Waco before I turned back. I just kept thinking I should never have let you do this."

"But how did you find us? I didn't give you the address."

"No, but you said it was near Fair Park. I drove around the area for about fifteen minutes without seeing your car. Then four Dallas cruisers zipped past me with sirens blaring. Somehow, I sensed you were in trouble, and I followed them, hoping I wasn't too late."

"You are definitely a sight for sore eyes," Deena said. "Wish you could've been here sooner and seen me in action."

He laughed. "I have no doubt you were amazing." He released his hold on them and stepped back when a homicide detective walked up and introduced himself.

At Maddy's questioning look, he grinned. "I'm not going anywhere until I make sure you're safe."

She smiled through the tears now threatening to spill over onto her cheeks as the realization that she and her sister had nearly died hit her like a truckload of bricks.

They were safe now, and in the process, they'd uncovered Agostinelli's real killer. Her life could get back to normal again. But now that Jake was here, she was definitely going to milk it for at least a day or two to keep him in Vineyard a while longer. At least until she figured out if there was anything between them. For now, she was just glad he was by her side.

* * * * *

Mike's funeral went smoothly although there were barely enough people there to fill the first three rows at St. Agatha's Church. Afterwards, the family gathered at Lainey's house to try to put a dent in the massive amount of food from the neighbors. Surprisingly, Deena had held up pretty well, considering she was burying her husband of eight years.

Now sitting around the dining room table, Maddy noticed the way the entire family seemed to be talking at once. She smiled, thinking it was one of the things she loved most about them. When her sisters got together, if one of them had something to say, they'd watch for someone to take a breath and then jump right in.

Her eyes connected with Jake's, and he smiled. Tomorrow he was leaving for San Antonio—again—but this time they'd made arrangements for him to come back to Vineyard to spend a few days with her and Jessie over the Christmas holidays. She remembered the way her daughter had squealed with delight when he'd told them.

She had no idea where their relationship was going, but right now she didn't care. She was having too much fun watching it develop.

He could be your new Dustbuster, Tessa said, sliding in beside her.

Maddy grinned, mouthing *thank you* to her sister's ghost.

No need to thank me. I just go where they tell me. And by the way, your face doesn't look too bad. Montero must hit like a girl.

Maddy tapped the table to get everyone's attention. "Wanted ya'll to know that Tessa's here."

"Hey, Tessa," Deena said. "We missed you earlier."

Tell her I don't do funerals. It reminds me too much of how dead I really am.

Maddy repeated Tessa's words, getting a laugh from her other sisters.

Tessa looked Deena's way. *How's she holding up?*

"She's good. Graveside services were a little tough on her, but we got her through it, and she's ready to get on with her life."

"Who are you talking to?" Jake asked, now looking at her as if she had a screw loose.

"You wouldn't believe me if I told you. Let's just say I have a pretend friend."

Lainey burst out laughing. "We all do. Even Colt. Hey, Tessa, are you staying around for awhile this time?"

Tessa shook her head. *I'm going to see if I can smooth things over with St. Pete's wife.* She shrugged. *Who knows? I may be back when you least expect it.*

"Oh God! I don't think I can handle any more adventures anytime soon," Maddy said, shaking her head. "And good luck with that St. Pete thing." She turned to the others and held up her hand. "Don't even ask."

Colt stood up and refilled everyone's coffee cup. When he got to Maddy, he stopped. "I still don't get why Agostinelli showed up at your house and talked to Jessie."

"I'm not sure, either, but I have a feeling it was part of the setup. Somehow, they got him to call my house at odd hours of the night looking for a man named Francis. In retrospect, I should have made a connection with the name when we went to Dallas to talk to Montero. My guess is they told Agostinelli the guy was there with the money." She paused to blow on the hot coffee and take a sip. "You have to admit, with all the evidence it would have been easy to convince a grand jury that I knew him."

"I'll say," Kate said. "And speaking of money, did they ever find the ten mil Agostinelli stole from the gangster?"

Colt shook his head. "No. The charges against Cavicchia were dropped, by the way, since Agostinelli could no longer testify. Montero did the mob boss a huge favor by whacking the accountant in his cell."

"Oh well. Guess we'll never know where he hid the cash. Sooner or later, though, they'll nab Cavicchia for something else. Everyone screws up sometime," Maddy said.

Lainey turned to Jake. "I hear we'll see you again at Christmas. Is that right?"

He nodded. "I wouldn't miss it for the world. I've never known a family that talks to an imaginary friend."

"Imaginary sister," Deena corrected. "And I wouldn't get on her bad side if I were you. Even dead she has a mean streak."

Jake laughed. "Oh boy! What am I getting myself into?"

He has no idea how crazy we really are, Tessa said before her expression turned serious. *I've got to go now, Maddy, and I don't know when I'll see you again.*

"You'll find a way," Maddy responded. "We all love you, Tessa."

I love you more, Tessa said before she disappeared.

"Is she gone?" Kate asked

"Yes, but I have the distinct feeling we haven't seen the last of her." Maddy looked upward and smiled when she heard Tessa's imitation of Arnold Schwarzenneger.

I'll be back.

About the Author

Photo by: Jane Harbin Helms

Liz Lipperman started writing many years ago, even before she retired from the medical field. Wasting many years thinking she was a romance writer but always having to deal with the pesky villains who kept popping up in all her stories, she finally gave up and decided since she read mysteries and obviously wrote them, why fight it? She's currently working on two mystery series--the Jordan McAllister Mysteries and The Garcia Girls Mysteries. You might also want to check out her romantic thrillers, Mortal Deception and Shattered. She wants readers to know that her G rated cozies are written as Liz Lippmann and her R rated, grittier mysteries as Lizbeth Lipperman.

She lives north of Dallas with her HS sweetheart hubby. When she's not writing she spends her time doting on her four wonderful grandchildren.

Other Books by Author

Writing as **Liz Lipperman**:

Clueless Cook Mysteries:
LIVER LET DIE
BEEF STOLEN-OFF
MURDER FOR THE HALIBUT

Jordan McAllister Mysteries:
CHICKEN CACCIA-KILLER
SMOTHERED, COVERED & DEAD - *novella*

Shorts:
CAN'T BUY ME LOVE - *short story*

Writing as **Lizbeth Lipperman**:

A Garcia Girls Mystery
HEARD IT THROUGH THE GRAPEVINE
JAIL HOUSE GLOCK
MISSION TO KILL

Romance:
MORTAL DECEPTION (a Romantic Mystery)
SHATTERED (a Romantic Thriller)

CPSIA information can be obtained
at www.ICGtesting.com
Printed in the USA
LVOW01s0004041016
507279LV00009B/84/P